Foundational Manhood

Building Your Life on Biblical Truth

Heath —

I pray this book will be a blessing to you & to Rose G.D has entrusted to your care — including your precious children & sweet bride. I love you, my brother!

Ryan Spry *Numbers 6:24-26*

Foundational Manhood: Building Your Life on Biblical Truth
Copyright© 2021 by Ryan Spry

All rights reserved. This book or any portion thereof may not be reproduced, stored in a retrieval system, transmitted in any form or by any means—electronic, mechanical, digital, photocopy, or any other—or used in any manner whatsoever without the express written permission of the publisher and author, except as provided by the United States of America copyright law.

ISBN: 978-8-72-656884-3 (softcover)

Printed in the United States of America—First Printing, 2021

Unless otherwise noted, all scriptures are from THE HOLY BIBLE, NEW INTERNATIONAL VERSION®. Copyright© 1973, 1978, 1984, 2011 by Biblica, Inc.™. Used by permission of Zondervan.

Scripture quotations marked (AMP) are taken from the AMPLIFIED® BIBLE, Copyright© 1954, 1958, 1962, 1964, 1965, 1987 by the Lockman Foundation. Used by permission. (www.Lockman.org). Scripture quotations marked (BSB) are taken from The Holy Bible, Berean Study Bible, BSB. Copyright© 2016 by Bible Hub. Used by permission. All Rights Reserved Worldwide. (www.berean.bible). Scripture quotations marked (CSB) are taken from the Christian Standard Bible®, Copyright© 2017 by Holman Bible Publishers. Used by permission. Christian Standard Bible•, and CSB® are federally registered trademarks of Holman Bible Publishers. Scripture quotations marked (CEV) are taken from the CONTEMPORARY ENGLISH VERSION, Copyright© 1995 by the American Bible Society. Used by permission. Scripture quotations marked (ESV) are taken from THE HOLY BIBLE, ENGLISH STANDARD VERSION®, Copyright© 2001 by Crossway, a publishing ministry of Good News Publishers. Used by permission. Scripture quotations marked (HCSB) are taken from the HOLMAN CHRISTIAN STANDARD BIBLE, Copyright© 1999, 2000, 2002, 2003 by Holman Bible Publishers, Nashville, Tennessee. All rights reserved. Scripture quotations marked (ISV) are taken from the INTERNATIONAL STANDARD VERSION, Copyright© 1996-2008 by the ISV Foundation. All rights reserved internationally. Scripture quotations marked (KJV) are taken from the KING JAMES VERSION, public domain. Scripture quotations marked (TLB) are taken from THE LIVING BIBLE, Copyright© 1971. Used by permission of Tyndale House Publishers, Inc., Carol Stream, Illinois 60188. All rights reserved. Scripture quotations marked (TM) are taken from THE MESSAGE: THE BIBLE IN CONTEMPORARY ENGLISH, Copyright© 1993, 1994, 1995, 1996, 2000, 2001, 2002. Used by permission of NavPress Publishing Group. Scripture quotations marked (NASB) are taken from the NEW AMERICAN STANDARD BIBLE®, Copyright© 1960, 1962, 1963, 1968, 1971, 1972, 1973, 1975, 1977, 1995 by The Lockman Foundation. Used by permission. Scripture quotations marked (NKJV) are taken from the NEW KING JAMES VERSION®, Copyright© 1982 by Thomas Nelson, Inc. Used by permission. All rights reserved. Scripture quotations marked (NLT) are taken from THE HOLY BIBLE, NEW LIVING TRANSLATION, Copyright© 1996, 2004, 2007 by Tyndale House Foundation. Used by permission of Tyndale House Publishers, Inc., Carol Stream, Illinois 60188. All rights reserved. Used by permission.

To our boys,

I thank God that He has entrusted you to the care of your mom and me, and I anticipate the moments when I can share with you about Jesus and how to live according to God's design for your lives.

My prayer is there will be plenty of opportunities when God will enable me to disciple you, share with you the love of Jesus, and model for you what it means to be a man of God.

No matter what the future holds, though, I want to ensure you are equipped with this knowledge, most importantly from the Bible, but also from experiences God has taken me through on my spiritual journey with Him.

This world is growing increasingly evil and resistant to Christianity, including mounting hostility toward those who follow Jesus. I implore you to accept Jesus as your Savior, so we will be with each other in Heaven forever and so you can meet the impending uncertainties with His strength.

You are so very precious to me, I have loved you infinitely since the moment we knew you were in your mommy's tummy, and I will always be so very proud of you!!

Daddy

Acknowledgments

First and foremost, I would like to thank God for the precious blood of my Savior, Jesus Christ, which atoned for my sins and secured for me eternal life. I am also grateful for His wisdom—that He gives generously without finding fault—as I penned this book.

I am also indebted to my beautiful bride, Amy, for her selfless dedication to combing through the pages of this text countless times to provide her honest feedback and gracious revisions. Amy, you are a blessing from God to me and our children, and I have been reminded of that daily as we navigated this process together.

To our boys, thank you for the motivation to finish this text in a God-honoring manner. My prayer is that this book will be a helpful resource to you, and if it ends up helping other men as well, I praise God that He used you coming into our lives as inspiration to reach others.

To our ministry and prayer partners, thank you for taking the time to provide your thoughts, prayers, and insight along this journey. I pray your families will be enriched by the truths God has placed on my heart to share in this text.

Lastly, thank you to those who have served as spiritual leaders and mentors in my life. I glean so much from you all on how to be a man after God's own heart, and I appreciate the leadership you provide to your spheres of influence that also sharpens me.

Table of Contents

Foreword   1

Where Were You When the World Stopped Turning?   3
   Disclaimer before Moving on   11

Part 1: Foundational Principles   15
   1. Salvation: My Sin Erased   17
   2. Sanctification: All Things New   23
   3. Victorious Living: Putting on the Armor   29
   4. Denying Self: Saying "Yes" to God   35

Part 2: Foundational Disciplines   41
   5. Daily Disciplines: What Do You Put in Your Mind?   43
   6. Bible Intake: Your Daily Bread   45
   7. Prayer: Your Steering Wheel or Your Spare Tire?   57
   8. Worship: To Whom or What is Your Praise Directed?   71
   9. Faith: Our God Never Fails   87

Part 3: Foundational Functions   99
   10. Spiritual Leadership: Christ's Ambassadors   101
   11. Husband: Prophet, Priest, and King   113
   12. Husbands, Recapture Your First Love!   125
   13. Father: Best-laid Plans   141
   14. A Father's Most Important Mission   147
   15. Worker: Not About Me   167
   16. A New Mission for Work   173
   17. Friend: Two are Better than One   185
   18. Steward: It's all God's   199

Burn the Ships   211

Notes   215

Foreword

We know God's way works because we've tried it both ways. The world's way—self-promotion, vain ambition, and scorekeeping—leaves you feeling empty, bitter, and joyless. God's way of dying to self and denying our flesh leads to peace and freedom. It's the opposite of what we would expect, but as Jesus said, "Whoever wants to save their life will lose it, but whoever loses their life for me will find it" (Matthew 16:25, NIV). The world around us is constantly saying that if you don't put yourself first, if you overlook a grievance, or if you set aside your wishes for the good of the other, that you will somehow end up with the deficit. But the opposite is true.

The Feminist movement has claimed to give women freedom from the oppression of submitting to anyone or anything, but I can say from experience that there is nothing more freeing than submitting to God's design for me and my husband's authority as he leads in the way described in this book. It is a true blessing as a wife to be taken care of, protected, and cherished. It is a beautiful thing "when the princes take the lead…" (Judges 5:2, BSB). Read this book, apply it, and watch your wife flourish under your covering. Your life will be better, her life will be better, your kids' lives will be better. And most importantly, God will be glorified!

—Amy Spry, Ryan's wife

INTRODUCTION

Where Were You When the World Stopped Turning?

I grew up in Houston, Texas for the first 15 years of my life. But the day after my ninth grade school year ended, my parents moved my younger brother and me to Andalusia, Alabama. To say I was a fish out of water would be a tremendous understatement. The high school I attended in Houston enrolled 3,700 students at the time of our move; the whole town of Andalusia had a population of 8,800. I moved from a city of four million residents to a state of four million. Admittedly, this move was not what I had planned for my life at such a formidable age. In His providence, however, God knew exactly what He was doing.

Back to my childhood in Houston for a moment. My family attended church, but we were not the type of people in church every time the doors were open. I vaguely remember attending a Sunday School class a time or two, but most of my memories of church attendance as a child center around being rather bored and uninterested during the hymns, doxologies, and sermons.

Because my mother grew up in the South (Mobile, Alabama to be precise), she made sure my brother and I were cognizant of our manners. Saying "yes, sir" and "yes, ma'am," opening doors for women, and thanking people for their help were attributes instilled in us at an early age. So, too, was the expectation we were to be respectful of authority and behave like "good" children. Anything less than compliance with these standards was met with my mouth being rinsed out with soap or having something—most likely my Nintendo—taken away from me for a period of time. I stress church attendance and being a "good" person here for a reason, which I will come back to later.

For now, let me continue unpacking God's providence in my life, and it started with love—or at least my idea of it as a teenager. The family of a girl I began to "date" attended a church down the road from the one where my family had joined. At the time, I noticed there was something different about this girl's family. For one thing, what I initially took away from meeting her father was that if I ever touched his daughter, he and I would spend some time together. For me, that time spent would be rather unpleasant. In one way, this man scared me; in another, my brash, big-city personality was such that I did not really care what he thought.

This girl's mother was a soft, sweet spirit who always welcomed me into her home, although I could tell she was not comfortable with the way I drove, the way her daughter and I spoke to each other from time to time, or the affectionate moments we spent on their front porch. Speaking of the front porch, her parents did allow their daughter to walk me out to the car—because very rarely did they let us venture out beyond their property lines—but if we were outside for too long, the front porch lights would start blinking…rather annoyingly, I might add. This level of parental involvement might have run off most teenage boys, but instead, God's providential hand kept me around this family for a season. For many reasons, I am so thankful He allowed me to do so.

As I mentioned, her parents were not too fond of their daughter going on dates with me, even though the only date that could be had in Andalusia was driving less than a mile down the road to the Dairy Queen. So to spend more time with her, I started going to church with her family. Honestly, my motives for attending their church were not pure. I wanted her parents to approve of me, and I thought going through the motions of their church activities would elicit their approval. However, as I began tuning into the messages being conveyed from the pulpit of that church, I started picking up on terms and phrases like "born again," "salvation," "eternal life," and "if you died today, are you sure you would go to Heaven"—terms that were foreign to me at the time. Nonetheless, I brushed them to the side as my focus remained on winning that girl's heart, as well as those of her father and mother.

Then one Tuesday morning, the rhetoric coming from that preacher all made sense. I was on some country backroads from Andalusia to Troy, driving way too fast around sharp curves in an attempt to make it to my college orientation class on time. About ten miles away from campus, news came across the radio airwaves that a small airplane—at least that is how the size of the airborne projectile was initially described—had hit one of the World Trade Center buildings. Thinking the radio station had taken a cruel joke too far, I turned the radio dial to another set of radio hosts who would not be inclined to joke about such grave events. Yet no quicker than my car antenna settled on their radio station did I hear a similar message from them: "a small aircraft has hit the World Trade Center."

Let me pause for a moment to remind our younger readers that cell phones were hardly in existence during this time (2001), and social media was several years out from being introduced to the masses. So instead of pulling out my phone to see who was live-tweeting the events occurring in New York City, I pressed my foot down even further on the accelerator to make it to campus in record time. Upon arriving at the classroom, some of my classmates were unaware of what was going on in our nation's largest city, as they had literally rolled out of bed, brushed their teeth (hopefully), and arrived just in time for class to begin. Yet their world, too, would be radically altered by the direct, succinct words uttered by our professor that morning: "The

World Trade Center has been struck by a plane. Please go home and be with your family."

If you know anything about a college campus, you know that if a faculty member cancels class, students rejoice. But this day was different. Instead of raising our hands in the air, high-fiving each other as we left the classroom, there was absolute silence. Our hearts hurt for those in the plane and the building, knowing there was a low chance of survival for any of them. Unfortunately, though, this was just the beginning of what would turn into a very long day. Before starting my hour-long journey home, I hurriedly paced down to the student center to see if any of the TVs were tuned into the coverage. It was then that I discovered a second plane had hit the South Tower and that this was no accident—it was a deliberate act of terror. Hours later, we would learn of another plane hitting the Pentagon and one more crashing into a field in Pennsylvania.

Once I arrived back home, I bypassed my parents and headed straight for my room, and for the rest of the day, my eyes and ears were locked into coverage of this national tragedy. I remember well I did not talk to anyone for the rest of that day. Instead, the same sobering thought kept coming to mind: "If you were in one of those towers and you did not make it out alive, you would not be going to Heaven." To be sure, on September 11, 2001, "it" all became clear. Every week, that small-town pastor had encouraged people to walk down the aisle and confess they needed certainty about their salvation. It turns out his—and ultimately God's—invitations were directed to me all along.

With no concern for the classes I would miss the next day, I reached out to the youth pastor, asking if we could go to lunch. Shortly after divulging to him all that had been going through my mind over the past 24 hours, I was in his office praying to accept Jesus Christ as my Lord and Savior. That Sunday, I made my profession of faith public, and a few weeks later, I was scripturally baptized as my first act of obedience to Jesus (Mark 16:16; Acts 2:38; Acts 10:48).

Ironically, the girl I was trying so hard to impress broke up with me soon after I was baptized. At the time, I was distraught and questioned God as to why this was happening. Author Steve Farrar refers to this sort of circumstance as a cross providence, which he defines as "any event occurring in your life where it looks like God is working against you."[1] As a teenager, it definitely felt like God was working against me, but in hindsight, I see the time spent with that precious family was yet another example of God's providence.

God used my time as a college student to do a few things: 1) to help me establish connections with leaders among the campus community who would help me obtain my first job in higher education, and more importantly, 2) to orchestrate the circumstances that resulted in me meeting my beautiful bride. Amy and I met while she was on our college campus for a visit. She says from that moment on, she knew in her heart that I was the type of man she desired to marry. Full disclosure—if she knew what was going through my mind at the time, I doubt the infatuation would have been as strong. Sure, I had my Bible laid open on my office desk, said all the right things, and seemed like I had it all together. Yet inside, there was no evidence of spiritual growth.

Most assuredly, my first season of life as a Christian was not the overnight conversion you may witness with some. Instead, it was much more of the same, only this time there was remorse when I did, said, thought, or acted the way I did (the work of the Holy Spirit in me). The youth pastor who led me to Christ gave me a short book that discusses the next steps for a new Christian, but the shininess of that book wore off rather quickly. And I think that speaks to a pervasive issue in the Church—we are often so consumed with helping others come to a saving relationship with Jesus Christ that we neglect what happens after their salvation. Indeed, my prolonged period as a spiritual infant is one of the reasons that initially prompted me to write this book.

Over the years that passed after our initial meeting, the relationship between Amy and I blossomed, and sure enough, she was right—she did marry someone like me…me! As the wedding grew closer, we began traditional pre-marriage counseling with Amy's childhood pastor. Our initial conversations were light in nature—who would hold the remote, who would do most of the cooking, and who would get to shower first in the morning. But as the meetings progressed, so, too, did the depth of the conversations. Specifically, the pastor began posing questions related to tithing, Bible study, and men leading the family. Remember that what I knew of maturing as a Christian was very limited to this point. Therefore, the magnitude of this concept of being the spiritual leader of the family did not really register with me. I just thought it meant making sure Amy was up to go to church each Sunday, which was an easy enough responsibility, considering she was a morning person. I laugh aloud as I type that, and as I do, I thank God for His mercy, grace, and patience with this slow learner!

Our marriage started out well enough. Both of us were employed, we were living in a new house, we experienced little to no bickering (except for one big spat about finances), and we were going to church most Sunday mornings. I was even incorporating some of the pastor's advice into my daily routine, as I began reading a chapter of the Bible each day (admittedly struggling with understanding what it meant) and praying with Amy occasionally. Even though I had begun adopting these new disciplines, there were still areas of my life that were not aligned with God's standards—TV shows that did not reflect a lifestyle of purity, alcohol consumption that impeded my ability to live a set-apart life, and language that did not honor a Holy King worthy of all my worship. (Again, so thankful to God for His patience with me!)

A couple of years into our marriage, I applied for a job in a nearby town. To be honest, I sought and eventually accepted the job because it would mean a 50 percent increase in my salary and gave no regard to whether God wanted us to make that move. Looking back, I again see God's hand of providence upon us, as this move was exactly what He intended. Several months after our move, Amy and I joined a church, and after some time as members, Amy was invited to join a women's Bible study led by some more seasoned ladies in the congregation. This study was the first in-depth study Amy had participated in—one that called for her to get up early in the morning to read and reflect on God's Word. As she established this newfound discipline of a daily quiet time, I noticed the quality of her character was growing as well. And as her walk with God strengthened, one big conviction was hanging over my head. God was shouting (this was no whisper): "YOU are supposed to be the spiritual leader, so why is Amy the only one growing in her walk with Me?" Whew, talk about something that cuts you deep.

Thankfully (and yet another example of God's providential nature), shortly after Amy joined this Bible study, there was another study beginning at our church—a journey through *MasterLife* by Avery Willis. If you are not familiar with this study, I highly, highly, highly recommend going through it. The first book of *MasterLife* introduces participants to daily disciplines to be cultivated in one's walk with God, while the second book focuses on how readers should slam the door to society's influences on the mind, will, and emotions (i.e., your "heart"). The third book reviews concepts of spiritual warfare, and the final book equips individuals to fulfill Jesus's Great Commission found in Matthew 28:16-20.[2] This 24-week, in-depth study is not for the faint of heart. There are five daily lessons per week, with each day of material taking about 20 to 30 minutes to read through. Willis challenges readers to memorize a verse or passage of Scripture each week, and there are several exercises those who go through the study are encouraged to complete. If I could illustrate for you what I felt as I began that study, imagine not being able to swim and being thrown into the deep end of a raging wave pool...stocked full of sharks. I was a spiritual infant trying to bite off a tough piece of meat, but I can tell you that it was absolutely worth it.

Never before had I been introduced to how I ought to posture myself to hear from God, how to have a vibrant quiet time, or why I continued to struggle with gratifying my sinful desires instead of being able to obey God. But after those 24 weeks, the picture came into focus. As a man called to be a spiritual leader to his family and those entrusted to him, there were a number of principles I needed to learn and cultivate to be the foundational man God expected me to be. Since that pivotal study, I have continued to pore over God's Word, other studies, and shelves full of literature to identify a set of foundational truths that will equip men to fulfill God's calling for their lives. Those principles are what I hope to unpack throughout this book, and I pray—upon completion of reading it—you will share the same enthusiasm I do for knowing God, glorifying Him, and making Him known to your sphere of influence. Are you ready to get started?

Disclaimer before Moving on

Years ago, birthed out of what I was seeing in our world, our nation, our churches, and our homes, I had the desire to write a book for men. But then God squelched my motivation for a season. Unbeknownst to me at the time, He hit the pause button for a couple of reasons:

1. To wait until my motives were pure and were wholly set on bringing Him glory; and
2. To orchestrate the timeline of completing this book to fall after the birth of our sons, so that I could write with them in mind.

To the former point, early in my ministry as a teacher of God's Word, part of my motivation was set on glorifying God, while the majority of my focus was set on glorifying myself. I'm embarrassed to confess I wanted others to know how much Scripture I could recite and how eloquent a speaker I was—all so I could get a pat on the back. God wants all of the glory (John 8:50), so I am thankful He had me take a step back to ensure this book was not about me, but rather all about Him!

To the latter point, when I first felt the tug to write a book for men, my wife and I did not have any children. We desperately wanted little ones, but God's timing was not yet right for us to be parents. In retrospect, I am grateful God delayed my writing of this book until our sons were born. I so strongly desire to see them grow up to be men of God that my enthusiasm for finishing this text in a God-honoring manner is stronger than ever before.

Now, before we jump in, let me take a moment to make a few other things abundantly clear from the beginning:

1. I am not perfect;
2. I am still learning; and
3. I need God's hand working in my life on a moment-by-moment basis.

You need to know these things because—like you—I have made mistakes. Like you, I do not know all there is to know about God and what He has purposed for my life (although the Bible gives us a pretty clear idea). Finally, like you, I am utterly dependent upon God to equip me, strengthen me, and empower me to fulfill His will. So, whether you are young in your spiritual walk, growing in your relationship with God, or a spiritually mature believer, my prayer is that you will use this book as a supplement to daily Bible reading as we unpack several principles, disciplines, and truths for foundational manhood together.

PART ONE

Foundational Principles

"By the grace God has given me, I laid a foundation as a wise builder, and someone else is building on it. But each one should build with care. For no one can lay any foundation other than the one already laid, which is Jesus Christ. If anyone builds on this foundation using gold, silver, costly stones, wood, hay or straw, their work will be shown for what it is, because the Day will bring it to light" (1 Corinthians 3:10-13a, NIV).

ONE

Salvation:
My Sin Erased

I spent a great deal of time articulating my testimony in the introduction for a few reasons. The first is I am convinced many men find themselves in a similar situation that I found myself in as a teenager—a "good" person going through the religious motions. You say all the right things, you do not cheat on your taxes or your wife, you attend church on Sundays, and you may even lead a Bible study group. But can I stress to you that *none* of that matters if you do not know Jesus Christ as your Lord and Savior?

Imagine that you are walking up to a cliff in the Grand Canyon and desire to travel over to the other side. You try to throw a rope across, but it falls short. You see a rotted-out bridge that will undoubtedly give out on you a few steps across the wide gap. Then you notice a bridge anchored deep into the ground that will assuredly grant you safe travels to the other side. Now, imagine your life and your eternal destination for a moment. Your good works are like the rope. Your church attendance and involvement are like the rotting bridge. Neither of these will grant you a safe and secure eternity. Only crossing to the other side on the well-anchored bridge by calling on Jesus to be your Lord and Savior restores your broken relationship with God and ensures your fellowship with Him forever in Heaven.

"Wait a minute," you may ask, "why is my relationship with God broken?" So glad you asked, as understanding this concept is essential to understanding your need for a Savior. Let me identify some key truths before I continue:

1. God is holy, and because of His holiness, He cannot tolerate anything to the contrary (Psalm 5:4).
2. God instructs us to be holy, as evidenced by His command to Moses to tell the people of Israel, "You shall be holy, for I the LORD your God am holy" (Leviticus 19:2b, ESV).
3. Consequently, when we are not living according to God's standard of holiness (i.e., perfection, without sin), we are disobedient.

So let's now explore what happens when we are disobedient to God's commands. In the first book of the Bible—Genesis—man (Adam) enjoyed fellowship with God until sin (i.e., disobedience) came along. As a consequence of this initial sin, "the LORD God banished him from the Garden of Eden to work the ground from which he had been taken" (Genesis 3:23, NIV). In other words, God said, "Adam, you disobeyed me, and now our relationship is broken."

As we progress through the first few books of the Bible, we see God provide a means by which man can *temporarily* restore proper fellowship with Him, and that was in the form of a sin offering at the annual Day of Atonement (Leviticus 4:1-5:13). On this day, the high priest would enter the Holy of Holies—an internal room of the tabernacle guarded by a thick veil or curtain. Before he entered, the high priest would make atonement for his own sins; then he would make atonement for the people's sins by presenting the prescribed sin offerings to God on their behalf (Leviticus 16).

This sacrificial system was a gift from God, but it was not a *permanent* fix to His people's sin issue. Therefore, in His infinite love, grace, and mercy, God sent into the world His only Son—Jesus Christ. By taking on the form of a human, Jesus would be the One who would live an obedient and sinless life, be offered as the eternal sin offering, conquer death through bodily resurrection three days after His last breath on the Cross, and forever tear down the veil figuratively and literally separating man from God.

If you have been in church for any length of time, you have probably heard Jesus's words from John 3:16 (NIV): "For God so loved the world that he gave his one and only Son, that whoever believes in him shall not perish but have eternal life." Jesus says in John 14:6 (NIV), "I am the way and the truth and the life. No one comes to the Father except through me." David says in Psalm 20:6-8 (NIV; emphasis added), "Now this I know: The LORD gives victory to his anointed. He answers him from his heavenly sanctuary with the victorious power of his right hand. *Some trust in chariots and some in horses, but we trust in the name of the LORD our God.* They are brought to their knees and fall, but we rise up and stand firm."

It grieves me to know many are trusting in their chariots and horses (i.e., good works) to get them into Heaven, when Jesus makes abundantly clear in the verses above that the only way to Heaven is through trusting in Him as Lord and Savior. Undeniably, those trusting in their good works will someday hear these words from Jesus: "Not everyone who says to me, 'Lord, Lord,' will enter the kingdom of heaven, but the one who does the will of my Father who is in heaven. On that day many will say to me, 'Lord, Lord, *did we not prophesy in your name, and cast out demons in your name, and do many mighty works in your name?*' And then will I declare to them, '*I never knew you; depart from me, you workers of lawlessness.*'" (Matthew 7:21-23, ESV; emphasis added).

As I close this section, I want to encourage you with some wisdom from Paul in Romans 5:8-10 (ESV): "God shows his love for us in that while we were still sinners, Christ died for us. Since, therefore, we have now been justified by his blood, much more shall we be saved by him from the wrath of God. For if while we were enemies we were reconciled to God by the death of his Son, much more, now that we are reconciled, shall we be saved by his life."

To put it simply, we are sinners, and God hates sin. Because He hates sin, the consequence of God's eternal wrath exists for all of humanity (Romans 3:23). But the beauty of the Gospel message is found in the latter part of Romans 6:23 (NIV; emphasis added): "the wages of sin is death, but *the gift of God is eternal life in Christ Jesus our Lord.*" Even while we were living sinful lives, God loved us so much that He extended an olive branch in the form of Jesus Christ to serve as the permanent sacrifice for our sins. We do not have to clean up our behavior before accepting Jesus as our Savior, nor do we have to perform a list of prescribed good works (e.g., giving, serving, teaching) before restoring our fellowship with God. All we have to do to be saved from God's wrath and secure eternity in Heaven with our Creator is "declare with your mouth, 'Jesus is Lord,' and believe in your heart that God raised him from the dead" (Romans 10:9, NIV).

So again, let me ask you to consider where you stand with God. Are you sure you have trusted in Jesus Christ as your Lord and Savior? Can you say without reservation that—if you died right now—you would spend eternity in Heaven with our Almighty God? Or would your sin sentence you to eternal punishment from our Creator? If there is ANY doubt, I implore you to pray something like this:

God, I confess to you that I am a sinner, and I certainly have not lived up to your standard of holiness in my life. I believe Jesus came into this world as the eternal High Priest and that He lived a perfect life, was offered as the eternal sacrifice for my sins, and was raised on the third day to defeat death and the grave. God, I want to be restored to fellowship with You and I want to be in Heaven with You, so I am calling on Jesus to be my Lord and Savior. Save me from my sins, fill me with your Holy Spirit, and help me to shed my former way of sinful living. May I keep my eyes fixed upon you as my Standard, so I may fulfill Your plans and purposes for my life.

Romans 10:13 (ESV) promises us that "everyone who calls on the name of the Lord will be saved." If you just prayed that prayer, I rejoice with you that you just made the best decision of your life! But now, I need you to know the second reason I shared my detailed testimony with you and that relates to what is next for your life—your sanctification.

TWO

Sanctification: All Things New

Our decision to call on and confess Jesus as our Lord and Savior is not the end of God working in us to be set apart for His good purposes—it is just the beginning. As much as it grieves me that there are so many men going through the religious motions and falsely assuming they will be in Heaven with God, it also pains me to know there are so many trusting in Jesus who remain living as spiritual infants for years. Many seem to think, "Well I have my salvation taken care of; now I can continue living the way I used to." Read God's words through Paul in Romans 6:1-4 (NLT) for a strong rebuke of that rationale:

> Well then, should we keep on sinning so that God can show us more and more of his wonderful grace? Of course not! Since we have died to sin, how can we continue to live in it? Or have you forgotten that when we were joined with Christ Jesus in baptism, we joined him in his death? For we died and were buried with Christ by baptism. And just as Christ was raised from the dead by the glorious power of the Father, now we also may live new lives.

Let us also consider Paul's words to the Corinthian church in 2 Corinthians 5:17 (NIV; emphasis added): "Therefore, if anyone is in Christ, the new creation has come: *The old has gone, the new is here!*" As the Bible makes clear, our old, sinful way of life is to be discarded once we have accepted Jesus as Lord of our lives, thereby allowing the process of spiritual maturity to take hold. Perhaps you have heard people refer to someone's salvation as being "born again" (a term coined by Jesus Himself in John 3:3). This concept of letting God shed you of the old way of living for a new standard (i.e., God's standard) is exactly what is being referred to with this terminology. So now for the remainder of this chapter, I want to address two common questions related to the process of sanctification: 1) what has changed that allows this transformation from the old way of life to a new way of living to manifest, and 2) what does this new way of living look like?

What has changed that allows this transformation from the old way of life to a new way of living to manifest?

Other than praying that prayer of salvation at the end of the last chapter (or whenever you confessed Jesus as Lord), you may be asking yourself what has changed in your life? Simply, EVERYTHING! Remember, God knows we cannot live according to His holy standards by ourselves, even after we accept Jesus as our Lord and Savior. Salvation is our positional righteousness with God, in that salvation gets us back into the correct posture and "position" for a proper relationship with God. However, God still expects us to live a life of obedience following our salvation—that is our practical righteousness.

To assist us with the latter, God gifted us with His Holy Spirit at the moment of our salvation to help us discern God's ways from our old, sinful ways. Jesus promises us in John 14:16 (ESV) that He "will ask the Father, and he will give you another Helper, to be with you forever." Earlier in John, chapter 7, verse 39 (NIV), Jesus speaks of living water flowing through us: "By this he meant the Spirit, whom those who believed in him were…to receive." Then in John 16:13a (NIV), Jesus affirms, "when he, the Spirit of truth, comes, he will guide you into all the truth." In other words, the Holy Spirit working in us is the One who will help us think holy thoughts, desire holy things, pursue holy endeavors, and be grieved when we commit an action that reflects our old way of living.

Please hear me—I need you to know you are not alone in this journey, nor does God expect you to live out your new life by yourself. Rather, it is the Holy Spirit equipping you with the power to live in a way that pleases and glorifies God (Acts 1:8). As we will discuss in the forthcoming chapters, we just have to be willing to deny ourselves of those old sinful tendencies daily and continually move forward in obedience to the Holy Spirit. The more we obey, the more aware we are of the Spirit's presence in our lives, which makes us increasingly sensitive to His leading—thus beginning a beautiful cycle the Bible refers to as fanning into flame the gift of the Holy Spirit (2 Timothy 1:6). That, men, is the process of sanctification.

What does this new way of living look like?

John succinctly answers this question in John 3:30 (ESV), when he states of Jesus in our lives, "He must increase, but I must decrease." In 2 Corinthians 3:18 (NLT; emphasis added), Paul states of those who are saved, "So all of us who have had that veil removed can see and reflect the glory of the Lord. And the Lord—who is the Spirit—makes us more and more like him as we are *changed into his glorious image.*" Quite simply, when we allow the Holy Spirit to work in us, our new way of living ought to reflect the life of our holy Savior, who is one with God the Father (John 10:30).

Practically speaking, there are 17 characteristics I want to share with you that exemplify Jesus's personality. According to T.W. Hunt, this set of qualities makes up the mind of Christ and originates from the following passages:[3]

> "[T]he wisdom that comes from heaven is first of all pure; then peace-loving, considerate, submissive, full of mercy and good fruit, impartial and sincere" (James 3:17, NIV).

"[T]he fruit of the Spirit is love, joy, peace, forbearance, kindness, goodness, faithfulness, gentleness and self-control. Against such things there is no law" (Galatians 5:22-23, NIV).

Below, there are two lists contrasting the 17 characteristics of Jesus (i.e., new standard of living) mentioned in the aforementioned passages, each beside its opposite quality (i.e., old way of living). As you read through these, pray God will open your eyes to any ways of darkness He wants to transform in you so that you may "Walk as children of light" (Ephesians 5:8, ESV).

New standard of living	Old way of living
1) Pure	1) Impure
2) Peace-loving	2) Causing a raucous
3) Considerate	3) Harsh
4) Submissive (accommodating; willing to yield)	4) Thinking you have it all figured out
5) Full of mercy	5) Cold-hearted
6) Full of good fruit	6) Stale; complacent
7) Impartial	7) Shows favoritism
8) Sincere (honest)	8) Manipulative
9) Love	9) Hate
10) Joy	10) Hopeless
11) Peace	11) Strife
12) Forbearance (patience)	12) Impatience
13) Kindness	13) Mean-spirited
14) Goodness	14) Evil
15) Faithfulness	15) Untrustworthy
16) Gentleness	16) Brash
17) Self-control	17) Out of control

You may have felt a sense of angst take over as you read this list, perhaps thinking there is no way you can achieve God's standard of living. (And you actually would be right, because without the Holy Spirit working in you, you cannot live this new way of life.) I felt the same way, but I have seen God faithfully help me change over the years from the old way of living to more closely resemble His new standard for me. Let my life and the lives of countless others be a testimony to you. When you begin cultivating the daily disciplines to be unpacked throughout this book, your desires, thoughts, words, and actions will start evolving to God's standards (Romans 12:2). Granted, we will never be perfect, but the Holy Spirit's work of sanctification in our lives ought to reveal growth, progression, and maturity as we reflect less of our old selves and more of our Savior to those we encounter—all for the glory of God.

THREE

Victorious Living:
Putting on the Armor

As you begin this sanctification journey, be warned. Our enemy, the devil, is cunning and loves to distort God's truth to make you doubt what you confess to believe, especially as you are actively seeking God's will for your life. Jesus says of the devil, "He was a murderer from the beginning, not holding to the truth, for *there is no truth in him*. When he lies, he speaks his native language, for *he is a liar* and *the father of lies*" (John 8:44, NIV; emphasis added). Below are some other verses from the Bible describing more of the devil's characteristics and tactics:

> "The thief comes only to *steal* and *kill* and *destroy*" (John 10:10a, NIV; emphasis added).

> "Be alert and of sober mind. Your enemy the devil *prowls around* like a roaring lion *looking for someone to devour*" (1 Peter 5:8, NIV; emphasis added).

> "Now the serpent was *more crafty* than any of the wild animals" (Genesis 3:1a, NIV; emphasis added).

> In Matthew 4:3 (NIV), the devil is referred to as "the tempter."

From these verses, we can easily surmise the devil is not one with whom we need to associate. He is a liar, a thief, a tempter, a stalker, a cunning serpent, and one without any truth in him. Furthermore, he speaks his native language (i.e., lies) to keep us from fulfilling God's purpose for our lives (Matthew 16:23), and he does so often through deceptive fallacies and myths that call into question what we believe to be true.

One of the areas where he tends to thrive is within our failures. Specifically, the enemy loves to convince us God will never forgive us for a particular thought, action, or word, and that we can never really be free from sins that so easily entangle us. Author Chuck Lawless says, "the enemy wants to rob us of our hope because he knows that a discouraged Christian is a defeated Christian."[4] Quite simply, the devil knows a defeated Christian man is of little use to God, and if we are convinced we cannot have victory over or forgiveness of our sin, we may wonder why we ought to bother trying to do so. This defeated mindset prompts the devil to subsequently claim victory and move on to the next man he can get to buy into his lies.

Here is God's rebuttal to this particular scheme of the devil. Yes, Romans 3:23 (NIV) says, "all have sinned and fall short of the glory of God," so we ought not to think that we are immune to sin. However, if we keep reading in the New Testament, we see that "If we confess our sins, he is faithful and just and will forgive us our sins and purify us from all unrighteousness" (1 John 1:9, NIV). Furthermore, to counter the lie that we will never have victory over a particular immoral behavior, be reminded: "You have been set free from sin and have become slaves to righteousness" (Romans 6:18, NIV). And again, in 2 Peter 2:9 (NIV), "the Lord knows how to rescue the godly from trials."

Do not miss this—at the moment you became a Christian, God freed you from the bondage of sin. As we discussed in the last chapter, He has empowered you (with the Holy Spirit working in you) to overcome your old, fleshly, sinful ways and live a life of righteousness for His glory. That is what you need to remember when the devil tries to tempt you to believe otherwise. Practically speaking, then, what do we do when we sin, and how can we experience God's forgiveness and victory over those actions?

Immediately confess, repent, and turn. Notice the word *immediately* here. I used to reserve my times of confession to God for my prayer time in the morning, often with the phrase, "Father, forgive me for where I have wronged and sinned against you." Sounds pretty "churchy," does it not? However, what I found was my prayers of confession and repentance were merely words. Admittedly, I was not truly grieved at my sin, because I was not confessing anything specific to Him—rather just speaking in generalities. It was then God impressed upon me the urgency to confess my sins as soon as they occurred, so 1) I would be less likely to forget the sins I had committed prior to my prayer time the next morning, and 2) I would have a strong conviction based on the specific error of my ways.

This latter point is an important one to consider, as it leads to genuine repentance. In the Old Testament, one of the Hebrew words (*nāḥam*) used for repentance means to feel sorrow.[5] Indeed, our sin against God ought to grieve us when we are on the path of sanctification. Keep reading in the Bible, and we find more of what God expects of a repentant man: "Repent therefore, and turn back, that your sins may be blotted out" (Acts 3:19, ESV). The Greek word for *repent* here is *metanoeō*, which means to "change one's mind for better...[and] heartily to amend with abhorrence of one's past sins."[6] Does it make you squeamish when you sin against God? Do you truly hate your sin? If we want to experience true freedom from the devil's attacks, we must be willing to hate our sins so much that we turn from those wicked ways, turn to God, and live a life honoring and glorifying Him.

Put on the spiritual armor. Do you know God has equipped you with the weapons needed to have victory over the devil? In Ephesians 6:11 (NIV), Paul refers to the "full armor of God," which can be used to "stand against the devil's schemes." These specific pieces of armor include the following:

- *Belt of truth*: to know Jesus, to know God's Word, and to live out the truths found in God's Word (James 1:22).
- *Breastplate of righteousness*: to live like Jesus (James 3:17; Galatians 5:22-23), to resist temptation (2 Corinthians 10:3-5), and to make right choices (1 Corinthians 8:1-13; 1 Corinthians 10:23-31).
- *Gospel shoes*: to stand ready and be on guard (1 Corinthians 16:13), to share the saving message of Jesus Christ with others (Matthew 28:16-20), and to be at peace with God and others (Romans 12:18).
- *Shield of faith*: to trust in God and not ourselves (Proverbs 3:5-6), to know He will provide an escape from our temptation (1 Corinthians 10:13), to believe He is always with us (Joshua 1:9), and to rest in Him as our Protector (Matthew 10:28-31).
- *Helmet of salvation*: to be aware of who we were before God saved us (Ephesians 2:1-3), to appreciate God's grace, to have an understanding of who we are in Christ (Romans 8; Ephesians 4:22; 2 Corinthians 5:17; Galatians 2:20), and to live with an eternal perspective (2 Corinthians 4:18; Luke 12:35-48).
- *Sword of the Spirit*: to read, meditate on, and apply God's Word, and to help others overcome the enemy's lies with Scripture.

My purpose for including an overview of these weapons here is so you know you have everything needed to defeat the devil and sin. For a more in-depth look at these truths, I strongly encourage you to complete the 7-week study entitled *Putting on the Armor: Equipped and Deployed for Spiritual Warfare* by Chuck Lawless, as some of these summaries came from that text.[7]

Move forward on the offensive. The spiritual armor is very much a defense mechanism for us, as we are able to use this weaponry to fight off attacks the devil hurls our way (Ephesians 6:10-18). In addition to being a good defense, though, putting on the spiritual armor allows us to live on the offensive. Notice the emphasized action verbs in the following verses:

> "Therefore *put on* the full armor of God, so that when the day of evil comes, you may be able to *stand* your ground, and after you have done everything, to *stand*" (Ephesians 6:13, NIV; emphasis added).

> "*Watch and pray* that you may not enter into temptation" (Matthew 26:41a, ESV; emphasis added).

> "*[T]ake up* the shield of faith, with which you can extinguish all the flaming arrows of the evil one" (Ephesians 6:16, NIV; emphasis added).

> "*Set* your minds on things that are above, not on things that are on earth" (Colossians 3:2, ESV; emphasis added).

> "So *flee* youthful passions and *pursue* righteousness, faith, love, and peace, along with those who call on the Lord from a pure heart" (2 Timothy 2:22, ESV; emphasis added).

So rather than just claiming victory over the devil, we employ these weapons to experience freedom and victory over him in advance of his tricks and schemes.

Jesus affirms that "If you hold to my teaching, you are really my disciples. Then you will know the truth, and the truth will set you free…So if the Son sets you free, you will be free indeed" (John 8:31-32, 36, NIV). Men, being set free from the bondage of sin begins with knowing Jesus, reading God's Word, and applying it to your life (the latter two concepts we will discuss in the forthcoming chapters). When we do so, we are more clearly able to recognize, confess, and turn from our sin, while we equip ourselves with God's defensive and offensive weaponry. When we implement these practices—although we will have momentary setbacks—we will experience freedom from our previous ways, freeing us up to glorify God with our new heart (Ezekiel 36:26). This journey starts with a simple, profound concept, but one that is immensely difficult to do—denying ourselves.

FOUR

Denying Self:
Saying "Yes" to God

Jesus says, "Whoever wants to be my disciple must deny themselves and take up their cross daily and follow me" (Luke 9:23, NIV). Merriam-Webster defines the term *disciple* as a "convinced follower of a school or individual."[8] Typically when you follow someone, you want to emulate their qualities, traits, and characteristics. Breaking down Jesus's words in Luke 9:23, then, if you are wanting to be a true disciple (emulator) of our Lord and Savior, you must deny yourself. This makes sense when we think back to our discussion on salvation. Man's natural inclination is toward sin; on the other hand, Jesus lived a perfect life without sin. Therefore, if we want to be like Jesus, we must deny our natural disposition toward sin.

So, what does this look like practically? Consider this example: I come home after a long, stressful day of work, and all I want to do is sit on the couch and watch football. Have you been there? However, my wife has also had a long day at home with two little boys and just needs some time to breathe for a moment. My natural impulse as a selfish, sinful man is to disregard her request and plop down on the couch for a few hours of uninterrupted television entertainment. Alternatively, denying myself and my selfish desires may look like me taking the boys outside for an hour after work, while my wife takes a bath and listens to her favorite podcast. It's not what I may immediately *want* to do—and it's certainly going to wear me out even more—but it is a practical way I can deny myself, lay down my life for the sake of my wife, and reflect the love of Christ to her in a tangible way.

Here's another illustration: you are out to lunch with some male colleagues, and your waitress catches your eye. She is beautiful, she is friendly, and she is available. In casual conversation, you happen to find out a little more about her, including her name. Fast forward to that evening when you and your wife engage in your third knock-down, drag-out argument of the week. This argument ends with doors slammed and you going your separate ways for the evening—her to the bedroom and you to the couch. In your anger and loneliness, your mind starts to wander to that beautiful waitress who was so friendly to you just hours before. Your natural desire is to look up the woman on social media and send her a message about how nice it was to meet her (rationalizing to yourself that you are just being a "nice guy" and complimenting her for her work). You may even suggest to her that you hope your paths would cross again soon. However, one message leads to another, and before you know it, you and she have talked online for hours, and you now have plans to go back to her restaurant tomorrow to see her again. You don't need an atlas to find where this path will lead you.

Denying yourself in this situation looks radically different. Rather than sleeping in separate rooms, a Spirit-filled man will make his way to the bedroom, initiate a conversation where he apologizes for his part in the argument, and then work toward resolution. It may not seem like it's the most pleasant thing to do at the time, but I can tell you the events that follow will be much more enjoyable than if you gratified the desires of your flesh with the waitress.

I want to share with you one real-life illustration before we move on. My father owned a land-planning business in Houston—one that attracted many developers in the region. In essence, land owners would give him a piece of land and ask him to design layouts for neighborhoods, shopping centers, and other developments. My mom was successful in her career, too, as she steadily worked her way up the corporate ladder at a large retail company over the years. A time came when she desired to take the next step in her career, moving from an assistant store manager to a position allowing her to manage her own store. But the promotion came with a catch—our family had to move nine hours east to Andalusia, Alabama, about which I have already painted a picture. Suffice it to say, there was not a lot of land development going on in that town. Nevertheless, my dad denied himself the potential for further professional growth so my mother could advance her career.

Jesus tells us in John 15:13 (NIV), "Greater love has no one than this: to lay down one's life for one's friends." To this date, every time I read that verse, my mind immediately jumps to three things: 1) Jesus and His obedience to death on the Cross, 2) our military and their sacrifices for our country's freedoms (thank you, troops), and 3) what my dad willingly gave up for my mother.

So you may be thinking, "This concept of denying myself sounds great in principle, but how do I get there?" Revert back to our discussion on the process of sanctification, and you will quickly find the answer to your question. By allowing the Holy Spirit to help you become more and more like Christ—the ultimate example of denying self to do our Heavenly Father's will (John 6:38)—in all you do, you will notice a spiritual progression from living for self to living for God. Please note, though, our goal in denying ourselves is for God alone to be glorified in our lives. Do not seek praise for your spiritual growth, as it is nothing you are doing, but rather what God is doing through you. Recall the words of Jesus when He says to His disciples, "Remain in me, as I also remain in you. *No branch can bear fruit by itself; it must remain in the vine.* Neither can you bear fruit unless you remain in me. I am the vine; you are the branches. *If you remain in me and I in you, you will bear much fruit; apart from me you can do nothing*" (John 15:4-5, NIV; emphasis added).

As I mentioned earlier, I fear the church focuses a good deal on getting lost souls saved, but the work of spiritual growth and sanctification is often left to the new believer to figure out on his own. And because of that, too many men are struggling in their own strength to deny themselves and live out holy lives, while never tapping into the transformational power of the Holy Spirit. Go back to Jesus's words in John 15:5 (NIV; emphasis added): "If you remain in me and I in you, you will bear much fruit; *apart from me you can nothing.*" In the next section, we will discover together what it means to remain in Jesus as we begin cultivating daily, practical disciplines that will help us grow closer in our walk with God. Come join me, won't you?

PART TWO

Foundational Disciplines

*"Have nothing to do with irreverent, silly myths.
Rather train yourself for godliness; for while bodily training is of
some value, godliness is of value in every way, as it holds promise
for the present life and also for the life to come"
(1 Timothy 4:7-8, ESV).*

FIVE

Daily Disciplines: What Do You Put in Your Mind?

The way we structure our daily routines is vitally important to our spiritual maturation. Here's why: there are 24 hours in a day and seven days in a week, which equates to 168 hours per week. Now, imagine the only time we are filling our minds with spiritual content is while we are sitting in the pew at church on Sunday morning (which is a big assumption, considering only 41 percent of Christians attend church weekly).[9] In this example, our Heavenly Father gets our minds for one hour, while the world (e.g., job, entertainment, hobbies, social media) captures the remaining 167 hours. Being generous and rounding up, God occupies .6% of our week (note the "." in front of the "6" there), while worldly influences (which we can agree are not generally aligned with God's Word) infiltrate the other 99.4% of our time. Do we still wonder why there is so much moral decay in our nation, our communities, and our homes?!? Perhaps now we can also understand why we cannot hear from God as well as we would like.

To put it plainly, whatever you put into your mind will affect your spiritual well-being. Granted, the forthcoming disciplines will not exempt you from worldly influences. However, when cultivated and practiced daily, these practices will chip away at the time the secular values of the world penetrate your heart, mind, will, and emotions. Moreover, I am confident that adding these precious moments with our Creator into your routine will enable you to know more of who He is, what He desires for your life, and how to live like Him, thereby glorifying Him in all you do. Acquiring this knowledge begins with our first daily discipline—reading, meditating on, applying, and memorizing the Bible. Let us read on together!

SIX

Bible Intake: Your Daily Bread

I have stated before that a big motivation behind writing this book was to serve as a "love letter" of sorts to our boys, giving them biblical knowledge, wisdom, and application for living according to God's standards. I love these little ones and want so desperately for them to experience, taste, and see the Lord *is* good (Psalm 34:8) and come to an understanding that His ways are far superior to the ways of the world. As much as I love our boys, though, the love I have for them pales in comparison to the love our Heavenly Father has for us. In fact, God so loved the world that He not only gave His one and only Son to save us from our sins (John 3:16), but He also used a host of ordinary people inspired by the Holy Spirit to pen 66 books that illuminate His path to holy and righteous living (Psalm 119:105). Assuredly, God Almighty was the first Author of love letters, and we are the benefactors.

Paul writes in 2 Timothy 3:16-17 (CSB; emphasis added), "All Scripture is inspired by God and is profitable for teaching, for rebuking, for correcting, for training in righteousness, *so that the man of God may be complete, equipped for every good work.*" Do you want to be set apart for righteousness? Do you want to allow the Holy Spirit to grow you more into the likeness of Jesus Christ? Do you want to glorify God? Start by opening the Bible.

Before I continue, I want to tell you why we should put such an emphasis on this discipline:

- The entirety of the Bible is God's holy inspired Word (2 Timothy 3:16).

- Since God—who is without error—is the Author of the Bible, every verse of His Word is also without error (Matthew 5:48; 2 Peter 1:20-21).
- The Bible is our instruction manual for holy and righteous living and should be our first source of wisdom before making a decision (2 Timothy 3:17; Psalm 119:105). We cannot pick and choose parts of the Bible to obey (James 2:10, TM). If I have a problem with God's Word, I am the problem.
- God Almighty and thus, the Bible, are our authority (Matthew 28:18), superseding any law, statute, rule, or worldview that the culture and its imperfect people concoct.
- God is in the past, the present, and the future (Revelation 1:8), so the Bible is just as relevant—and will continue to be as relevant—as it was when it was first written.

Reading God's Word

As you begin—or look to enhance—this daily discipline, I would make two things a priority. The first is to read God's Word in its entirety at least once. As I mentioned before, the Bible is God's love letter to you. We wouldn't ignore reading sections of a love letter our spouse wrote to us, so why do we feel like we can do so with God's love letter to us? I have heard arguments that the Old Testament is no longer relevant, boring, or difficult to read through. I would encourage those who may think those thoughts to not omit any part of the Bible, as every page contains details of God's redemptive plan for His people. If you need assistance on how to begin reading the Bible, please know there are plenty of helpful resources and reading plans available at your fingertips to get you started. No matter how you begin, though, the important first step is to open God's Word, start reading, and allow Him to speak to you.

The other Bible-reading priority I would encourage you to implement is reading a chapter from the book of Proverbs every day. I am forever grateful for the insight Pastor Johnny Hunt shared with a group of men at one of his annual conferences, as he gave us a glimpse into his daily Bible reading time. Hunt told attendees he reads a chapter of Proverbs each day and began to explain how much practical wisdom he gleaned from his time in this particular book of the Bible.[10] Let me share with you some of my favorite verses from Proverbs (all ESV) that I have cherished over the past several years of cultivating this daily practice:

> "Hear, my son, your father's instruction, and forsake not your mother's teaching" (1:8).

> "For the LORD gives wisdom; from his mouth come knowledge and understanding; he stores up sound wisdom for the upright; he is a shield to those who walk in integrity" (2:6-7).

> "Honor the LORD with your wealth and with the firstfruits of all your produce; then your barns will be filled with plenty, and your vats will be bursting with wine" (3:9-10).

> "Do not enter the path of the wicked, and do not walk in the way of the evil" (4:14).

> "[T]he lips of a forbidden woman drip honey, and her speech is smoother than oil, but in the end she is bitter as wormwood, sharp as a two-edged sword" (5:3-4).

> "A little sleep, a little slumber, a little folding of the hands to rest, and poverty will come upon you like a robber, and want like an armed man" (6:10-11).

> "Say to wisdom, 'You are my sister,' and call insight your intimate friend, to keep you from the forbidden woman, from the adulteress with her smooth words" (7:4-5).

"Hear instruction and be wise, and do not neglect it" (8:33).

"The fear of the LORD is the beginning of wisdom, and the knowledge of the Holy One is insight" (9:10).

"Whoever walks in integrity walks securely, but he who makes his ways crooked will be found out" (10:9).

"Whoever trusts in his riches will fall, but the righteous will flourish like a green leaf" (11:28).

"Lying lips are an abomination to the LORD, but those who act faithfully are his delight" (12:22).

"Whoever walks with the wise becomes wise, but the companion of fools will suffer harm" (13:20).

"Whoever is slow to anger has great understanding, but he who has a hasty temper exalts folly" (14:29).

"Without counsel plans fail, but with many advisers they succeed" (15:22).

"Pride goes before destruction, and a haughty spirit before a fall" (16:18).

"Whoever mocks the poor insults his Maker; he who is glad at calamity will not go unpunished" (17:5).

"Before destruction a man's heart is haughty, but humility comes before honor" (18:12).

"Listen to advice and accept instruction, that you may gain wisdom in the future" (19:20).

Bible Intake: Your Daily Bread

"Wine is a mocker, strong drink a brawler, and whoever is led astray by it is not wise" (20:1).

"The horse is made ready for the day of battle, but the victory belongs to the LORD" (21:31).

"A good name is to be chosen rather than great riches, and favor is better than silver or gold" (22:1).

"Let not your heart envy sinners, but continue in the fear of the LORD all the day" (23:17).

"Do not rejoice when your enemy falls, and let not your heart be glad when he stumbles, lest the LORD see it and be displeased, and turn away his anger from him" (24:17-18).

"A word fitly spoken is like apples of gold in a setting of silver" (25:11).

"Like a dog that returns to his vomit is a fool who repeats his folly" (26:11).

"Let another praise you, and not your own mouth; a stranger, and not your own lips" (27:2).

"Whoever gives to the poor will not want, but he who hides his eyes will get many a curse" (28:27).

"Do you see a man who is hasty in his words? There is more hope for a fool than for him" (29:20).

"If you have been foolish, exalting yourself, or if you have been devising evil, put your hand on your mouth" (30:32).

"Her children rise up and call her blessed; her husband also, and he praises her: 'Many women have done excellently, but you surpass them all.'" (31:28-29).

These verses are just the beginning of the wisdom you can gather from reading a chapter from the book of Proverbs each day; I highly recommend it!

Meditating on God's Word

Not only is it important for us to open God's Word to receive instruction from Him, but we must also make concerted efforts to study and meditate on His precepts outlined in Scripture. Consider the following verses:

> "Blessed is the man who walks not in the counsel of the wicked, nor stands in the way of sinners, nor sits in the seat of scoffers; but his delight is in the law of the LORD, and on his law he *meditates* day and night" (Psalm 1:1-2, ESV; emphasis added).

> "This Book of the Law shall not depart from your mouth, but you shall *meditate* on it day and night, so that you may be careful to do according to all that is written in it. For then you will make your way prosperous, and then you will have good success" (Joshua 1:8, ESV; emphasis added).

The Hebrew word for *meditate* in these two passages denotes a picture of rumination, whereby a cow chews its cud. If you do not know much about livestock, let me share with you some insight into this digestive process. When cows chew the cud, food is swallowed, regurgitated back up, then chewed and swallowed again. Within this process, the cow is experiencing the food over and over.

Let me offer a contrasting illustration for you: when our family dog was still with us, one of the last remaining joys of his life was when we ate steak for dinner. He never otherwise begged for food at the table, but any time he smelled steak on the table, his nose was in my lap waiting for a bite of this delicious meat. And typically, I offered him my final two bites of steak right off the fork (he had become a spoiled, high-maintenance dog in his old age). Despite his anticipation of those last few bites from my plate, however, he swallowed the meat so quickly that there was hardly any time to taste it.

Now, imagine yourself sitting down at the dinner table, and in front of you, your bride has made your favorite meal. If you are like me, you will savor every bite, letting it linger in your mouth as you take precious time to experience and enjoy the meal before you. Men, I want to encourage you to approach your time with God's Word in a similar manner. You should not be like our family dog—scarfing down a fine piece of meat without hardly tasting the bite—but rather like the cow, ruminating on those sweet moments when God is speaking to you through His holy inspired word.

I don't find it a coincidence the Executive Pastor of our church carved out a section of his sermon to speak on this topic while I was writing this chapter. In his message, he offered five practical steps to help us get started meditating on our daily readings from the Bible:

- S: Is there **sin** to confess?
- P: Is there a **promise** to claim?
- E: Is there an **example** to follow?
- C: Is there a **command** to obey?
- S: Is there a **stumbling block** to avoid?[11]

It does not matter what method you employ as you begin meditating on specific verses or passages—just begin doing so!

Applying God's Word

One of the common missteps in our daily walk with God—myself included—is we read some beautiful principles in the Bible and may even take some time to reflect on that wisdom, but just as soon as we close the cover, we forget about what we have read and go on with our daily routines. James exhorts readers in James 1:22 (CSB) to "be doers of the word and not hearers only, deceiving yourselves."

In other words, do not approach your time reading the Bible as another task to be checked off your to-do list. Instead, take time to read it, study it, meditate on it, AND apply it, letting it transform you into a man after God's heart. Otherwise, you are fooling yourself into thinking you have it all together when in reality you are just flippantly approaching God's Word as just another book on your shelf.

Furthermore, ignoring the standards by which God desires for you to live—after being introduced to these truths in His Word—is sin. Don't believe me? Look back at the book of James for proof: "whoever knows the right thing to do and fails to do it, for him it is sin" (4:17, ESV).

Memorizing God's Word

Jesus was weary; He was hungry; He was undoubtedly exhausted. He had just completed a 40-day fast. It was then the devil came to our Savior, tempting Him. Let's read the account from Matthew 4:3-11 (NIV):

> The tempter came to him and said, "If you are the Son of God, tell these stones to become bread."
> Jesus answered, "It is written: 'Man shall not live on bread alone, but on every word that comes from the mouth of God.'"
> Then the devil took him to the holy city and had him stand on the highest point of the temple. "If you are the Son of God," he said, "throw yourself down. For it is written:
>> "'He will command his angels concerning you,
>> and they will lift you up in their hands,
>> so that you will not strike your foot against a stone.'"
>
> Jesus answered him, "It is also written: 'Do not put the Lord your God to the test.'"

> Again, the devil took him to a very high mountain and showed him all the kingdoms of the world and their splendor. "All this I will give you," he said, "if you will bow down and worship me."
> Jesus said to him, "Away from me, Satan! For it is written: 'Worship the Lord your God, and serve him only.'"
> Then the devil left him, and angels came and attended him.

What I want you to get out of this passage is the model by which we ought to fend off temptation. Notice, every time "the tempter" tempted Jesus, His reply was not one of trying to reason with the devil. Rather, Jesus replaced the devil's enticements with God's Truth, reciting Deuteronomy 8:3, 6:16, and 6:13 respectively. So I have a question for you to consider—if the Son of God thought it appropriate and wise to refute the devil's attacks by recalling Scripture, shouldn't we think it appropriate and wise to do so as well?

In Psalm 119:11 (ISV), the Psalmist proclaims of God's Word, "I have stored what you have said in my heart, so I won't sin against you." Is there a specific temptation with which you struggle? Wise men will take time to memorize a Bible verse or two to remember when they are vulnerable. For instance:

- Lust: "You are not to desire your neighbor's wife" (Deuteronomy 5:21a, ISV).
- Greed: "For the love of money is a root of all kinds of evils" (1 Timothy 6:10a, ESV).
- Gossip: "Let no corrupting talk come out of your mouths, but only such as is good for building up, as fits the occasion, that it may give grace to those who hear" (Ephesians 4:29, ESV).
- Judging: "Do not judge, or you too will be judged. For in the same way you judge others, you will be judged, and with the measure you use, it will be measured to you" (Matthew 7:1-2, NIV).

- Anger: "Everyone should be quick to listen, slow to speak, and slow to anger" (James 1:19b, CSB).
- Not willing to forgive: "Bear with each other and forgive one another if any of you has a grievance against someone. Forgive as the Lord forgave you" (Colossians 3:13, NIV).

As I have encouraged men to incorporate this practice into their daily spiritual journey, I have heard every excuse in the book: "I'm too old to memorize verses"; "I don't have enough time to focus on this"; "I can never remember the verse when the temptation comes"; "My memory is horrible"; and so much more. If you find yourself saying something similar, tell me the lyrics of your favorite song—just a line or two. Or perhaps the score of last night's game. Or exactly where you were when you heard the news President Kennedy had been assassinated, the Challenger Space Shuttle exploded, or two planes hit the World Trade Center towers. Chances are, you can recall one or more of these items rather easily, so I ask you, what is holding you back from memorizing the most important knowledge you can possess—knowledge that will help you reject the devil's lies and fend off temptation?

Early on in my walk with God, I would often struggle with knowing God's plans, purposes, and will for my life. Perhaps you are there now. Yet as I began opening up God's Word, meditating on His truths, applying the Bible to my life, and committing to memory specific verses that would help me overcome the devil's tactics, God's design for my life became so much clearer. I assure you that if you take time to implement this discipline, it will make a considerable difference in your sanctification journey. For example, meditating on the story of Joseph fleeing from Potiphar's wife could prompt you to make the application you need to flee from that "friendly" relationship you have been having with a co-worker.

As we will unpack in a bit, God intends for us to reflect the image of our Savior to those we encounter, so He alone will be glorified (2 Corinthians 5:20; 1 Corinthians 6:20). Show me a man who you think to be a Godly man and glorifies God in his life, and I would be willing to bet he is a student of Scripture!

Questions to Consider

1. In what area(s) does the devil tempt you?

2. What verse(s) can you memorize to replace those lies with God's Truth?

SEVEN

Prayer:
Your Steering Wheel or Your Spare Tire?

For those who are married, think back to when you and your wife were dating. I know for me, I wanted to spend a lot of time talking to Amy—finding out what she liked, learning more about her background, and discovering all of her fears, hopes, and dreams. In fact, there were times I recall us talking over the phone so late into the night that one of us would end up falling asleep while still connected. Honestly, I could not find enough time in the day to talk to this woman with whom I was falling in love. After almost 15 years together, it still absolutely brightens my day to be able to hear from and talk to her regularly. But here is my conviction: why do I not have the same zeal and passion to hear from and speak to God, who loves me infinitely more than Amy does?

Talking to God during times of prayer is our opportunity to communicate with God: to adore Him for who He is, to confess our failures, to tell Him our fears, anxieties, and worries, to petition Him with our needs, and to listen in the stillness of the moment for His voice. In these moments, we can discern His prompting, His direction, and His correction for our lives.

Despite its many benefits, this discipline is a commonly overlooked aspect of our daily walk with God for several reasons. First, we do not think we have time for prayer. Second, we simply do not know where to start or how to begin our prayer time. Finally—and most unfortunately—we do not see the benefit of an effective prayer time with God.

To the former, let me share with you a quote from author Ryan Blair, who says, "If it is important, you'll find a way. If it's not, you will find an excuse."[12] For those who enjoy college football, when was the last time you missed your favorite team play? For those who love to eat, when was the last time you missed a meal? For those who love to hunt, when was the last time you missed going out into the deer stand or duck blind? If you are finding it hard to carve out time to pray, may I encourage you to wake up 10 minutes earlier, go to bed 10 minutes later, or set aside something less important (your phones, for example) for 10 minutes so you can commune with God. I promise that you will not regret it. (By the way, there is nothing magical about 10 minutes of prayer, but it is a good foundation from which to begin.)

To those struggling with how to begin your prayer time, I would like to share with you some insight on how I structure my daily communication with God. There are many other prescribed methods for prayer available, so like the Bible reading plans I mentioned in the last chapter, find a system that works for you. For me, I like to use the A.C.T.S. method of prayer, starting with **adoration**—praising God for who He is. (Just as an aside: we learn more about who God is by reading His Word, which then leads to a clearer understanding of how to praise Him.) There are so many attributes to God's character that there is not enough space for me to list them all here (or in my prayer time), so I like to start from the beginning of the alphabet each day and work my way through to the end. Something like the following list of qualities is what I lift up in praise to God on a daily basis:

- Almighty (Revelation 1:8, NIV)
- Bountiful (Psalm 13:6, ESV)
- Comforter (2 Corinthians 1:3-4, NIV)
- Deliverer (Psalm 18:2, CSB)
- Eternal (Psalm 90:2, AMP)
- Faithful (1 Corinthians 10:13, NIV)
- Generous (James 1:5, NASB)
- Holy (Psalm 99:9, NLT)
- Immovable (Psalm 144:1, TLB)

- Just (Deuteronomy 32:4, NIV)
- Kind (Titus 3:4, ESV)
- Loving (1 John 4:8, NLT)
- Miracle Worker (Psalm 77:14, NIV)
- Name above all names (Philippians 2:9, KJV)
- Omnipotent (Psalm 147:5, CSB)
- Provider (Philippians 4:19, ESV)
- Quickener (John 6:63, KJV)
- Righteous (Psalm 145:17, NIV)
- Sovereign (Isaiah 61:1, NIV)
- Triumphant (2 Corinthians 2:14, NLT)
- Unchanging (Malachi 3:6, ESV)
- Valiant (Psalm 118:16, CSB)
- Wonderful (Psalm 145:3, CEV)
- eXalted (1 Chronicles 29:11, NIV)
- Yearning (James 4:5, ESV)
- Zealous (Isaiah 59:17, NIV)

A couple of things occur as I progress through this initial stage of prayer. For one, I gain a better appreciation and understanding of who God is, which gives me greater confidence as I offer prayers of petition and supplication later. For instance, if I am praying for provision for a friend of mine, I can confidently make that request to the Provider. Or, if I am praying for someone who has just lost their spouse, I can lean on the Comforter to help that grieving widow. Secondly, when recognizing God for who He is, I see myself for who I am. Read the prophet Isaiah's words: "'Woe to me!' I cried. '*I am ruined*! For *I am a man of unclean lips*, and I live among a people of unclean lips, and my eyes have seen the King, the LORD Almighty'" (Isaiah 6:5, NIV; emphasis added).

Just like Isaiah, recognizing who I am (a man of unclean lips) before a holy God leads naturally into the next stage of prayer—**confession**. As we discussed before, any time you become aware that you have sinned, you should immediately turn to God in repentance. However, this should also be an aspect of your daily prayer discipline.

Some may ask why we need to confess our sins when God has already forgiven us, so let me offer this rebuttal from Psalm 66:18 (NLT): "If I had not confessed the sin in my heart, the Lord would not have listened." The latter stages of my daily prayer time are devoted to making my requests known to God. I don't know about you, but I would like for Him to not turn away when I am making those appeals.

When you enter into this time of confession, I challenge you to do a few things: 1) ask God to search you and reveal any way displeasing to Him (Psalm 139:23-24), 2) be specific about the sins you have committed, 3) ask for forgiveness from your disobedience, and 4) ask God to cleanse you from your unrighteousness and create in you a clean heart and renewed spirit for obeying Him. First John 1:9 (NIV) states, "If we confess our sins, he is faithful and just and will forgive us our sins and purify us from all unrighteousness." That is something for which we can be thankful, which leads into the subsequent aspect of prayer—**thanksgiving**.

I vividly remember whenever I received a birthday or Christmas gift as a child, my first step afterward was not to begin playing with the item. Rather, I was tasked by my mom with writing a note to the giver of that gift, expressing my appreciation for their generosity. Admittedly, some of my notes were more heartfelt than others—depending upon how much I valued the gift I received. Well, the most important gift you and I have ever received is the "gift of God" that "is eternal life in Christ Jesus our Lord" (Romans 6:23, NIV), and every day, we should thank God for that gift.

My prayers of thanksgiving do not stop there, however, as I go on to thank God for: His Holy Spirit; His Word; the people He has entrusted to my care (i.e., wife, children, family, friends, colleagues, ministry partners, neighbors); the home, cars, and jobs He has given to us; health; safety; our church; and on and on and on. I stumbled upon a convicting quote recently in regards to this spirit of thankfulness that resonated with me: "What if you woke up today with only the things you thanked God for yesterday?"[13] Granted, I do not think God is in Heaven keeping a list of things we do or do not thank Him for, but I still would like to join joyfully with the Psalmist, who intends to "Enter his gates with thanksgiving, and his courts with praise!" (Psalm 100:4, ESV).

After I have praised God by telling Him all the ways I adore Him, confessed my sins and shortcomings to Him, and thanked Him for His many blessings and provisions, I enter into my final stage of prayer—**supplication** (and intercession) for all the saints (Ephesians 6:18, ESV). Here, I offer specific requests to God for myself (supplication) and others (intercession). Prayers for provision, healing, protection, and much more are included during this time of supplication and intercession.

As you consider this portion of your own prayer time, take note that this list of prayer requests can get overwhelming (particularly if you are in tune with the needs of others). To help you overcome that sense of anxiety, I would like to offer another suggestion to you—a system within the system, if you will. I would encourage you to section off your prayers for individuals and people groups into specific days of the week. For instance, Sunday mornings could be spent praying for the upcoming church service, as well as protection over and wisdom for your church staff. On Mondays, you may pray for your colleagues as you start your work week. Tuesdays could be spent praying for your extended family (your wife and children should be included in your daily prayers of intercession). On Wednesdays, you could pray for your ministry partners or Sunday School members, and so on. In sum, develop a structured—yet not a rote—prayer strategy that works for you, but most importantly, gets you closer to the One who cares about and supplies your every need (Philippians 4:19).

Before moving onto our next spiritual discipline, I want to leave you with a few more points of consideration as it relates to prayer.

Pray about everything. In Joseph Scriven's famous hymn, "*What a Friend We Have in Jesus*," we sing these words:

> Oh, what peace we often forfeit,
> Oh, what needless pain we bear,
> All because we do not carry
> Everything to God in prayer![14]

You may have doubts God really cares about the small things in your life. Or, maybe you think you can handle those small things on your own, so you only pray about those big-ticket items seeming to weigh you down. Yet Paul says in Philippians 4:6-7 (NLT; emphasis added) to not "worry about anything; instead, *pray about everything*. Tell God what you need, and thank him for all he has done. *Then you will experience God's peace*, which exceeds anything we can understand. His peace will guard your hearts and minds as you live in Christ Jesus." Even those minor things you think you can handle are important to God and are causing you some level of anxiety. Small worries build on top of one another to create a broader sense of stress, so why not obey God, take everything to Him, and experience His peace?

Pray continually. Paul tells us in 1 Thessalonians 5:17 (ESV) to "pray without ceasing." Too often, though, I find myself falling into the trap of spending time conversing with God before I start my workday, but then during and after work, not a word is uttered to Him. When I need Him the most throughout my day, my natural tendency is to go at it alone and rely on myself. Do not let the devil convince you this is OK. We need God every moment of the day. We are totally dependent on Him for every breath we take, every meeting we have, every phone call we take, and everything in between. Take time to pray short prayers of petition that God would be glorified during these moments, and by doing so, acknowledge your complete dependence on Him.

Do not feel like you have to do all the talking. When done effectively, communication is a two-way street—one person conversing with another. Think about your time spent at work; you probably do not want to be supervised by someone who never asks for your input. So why do we approach God in a similar way as that boss and feel like we have to do all the talking? Some of my greatest moments of prayer occurred when I let my needs be known to God, then waited in silence on a response from His Holy Spirit.

Do not make a spectacle out of praying. God is not impressed with a bunch of hollow words lifted up to Him. Read Jesus's rebuke in Matthew 6:5-7 (ESV; emphasis added) for evidence of this:

> And when you pray, you must not be like the hypocrites. For they love to stand and pray in the synagogues and at the street corners, that they may be seen by others. Truly, I say to you, they have received their reward. But *when you pray, go into your room and shut the door and pray to your Father who is in secret.* And your Father who sees in secret will reward you. And *when you pray, do not heap up empty phrases as the Gentiles do, for they think that they will be heard for their many words.*

Your Father in Heaven knows your needs before you ask Him (Matthew 6:8), so do not fall for the devil's lie when he tries to convince you that you need to be the most articulate, well-versed orator for your prayers to be heard and answered. First Peter 5:5b (CSB) says, "God resists the proud, but gives grace to the humble." Which side of the fence do you want to be on when petitioning God with your requests?

Ask with the right motives. James 4:3 (ESV) declares, "You ask and do not receive, because you ask wrongly, to spend it on your passions." Let me challenge you to do some introspective thinking this week and consider why you are asking God for certain things. Are you asking Him for provision so you can enjoy a more lavish lifestyle, or do you anticipate being able to use those extra funds to begin a ministry at church that God has put on your heart? Are you requesting relief from an inconvenience (e.g., person, illness, situation) for your comfort, or are you asking for something that you are convinced is aligned with God's will and will bring Him glory? Answers to these questions may reveal why the responses you receive from God are not what you desire.

Believe God to answer prayer. Jesus says in Mark 11:23-24 (NIV), "Truly I tell you, if anyone says to this mountain, 'Go, throw yourself into the sea,' and does not doubt in their heart but believes that what they say will happen, it will be done for them. Therefore I tell you, whatever you ask for in prayer, believe that you have received it, and it will be yours." As you read through the Bible, you will notice God has done some amazing things—things only an All-powerful, Almighty God could do. Be encouraged by God accomplishing the impossible, and pray in faith for God to move mountains on your behalf, just like famous evangelist George Müller did on his way to a speaking engagement. The story is told of Müller by Charles Inglis:

> When I first came to America, thirty-one years ago, I crossed the Atlantic with the captain of a steamer who was one of the most devoted men I ever knew, and when we were off the banks of Newfoundland he said to me:
>
> "Mr. Inglis, the last time I crossed here, five weeks ago, one of the most extraordinary things happened which has completely revolutionized the whole of my Christian life. Up to that time I was one of your ordinary Christians. We had a man of God on board, George Müller, of Bristol. I had been on that bridge for twenty-two hours and never left it. I was startled by someone tapping me on the shoulder. It was George Müller…"
>
> "Captain," he said, "I have come to tell you that I must be in Quebec on Saturday afternoon." This was Wednesday.
>
> "It is impossible," I said.
>
> "Very well, if your ship can't take me, God will find some other means

of locomotion to take me. I have never broken an engagement in fifty-seven years."

"I would willingly help you. How can I? I am helpless."

"Let us go down to the chart-room and pray."

I looked at that man of God, and I thought to myself, what lunatic asylum could that man have come from? I never heard of such a thing.

"Mr. Müller," I said, "do you know how dense the fog is?"

"No," he replied, "my eye is not on the density of the fog, but on the living God who controls every circumstance of my life."

He got down on his knees and prayed one of the most simple prayers. I muttered to myself: "That would suit a children's class where the children were not more than eight or nine years old." The burden of his prayer was something like this: "O Lord, if it is consistent with Thy will, please remove this fog in five minutes. You know the engagement you made for me in Quebec Saturday. I believe it is your will."

When he finished, I was going to pray, but he put his hand on my shoulder and told me not to pray. "First, you do not believe He will; and second, I believe He has. And there is no need whatever for you to pray about it." I looked at him, and George Müller said, "Captain. I have known my Lord for fifty-seven years, and there has never been a single day that I have failed to gain an audience with the King. Get up, captain, and open the door, and you will find the fog is gone." I got up, and the fog was gone! On Saturday afternoon, George Müller was in Quebec.[15]

Jesus tells His disciples in Matthew 19:26 (CSB; emphasis added), "With man this is impossible, but *with God all things are possible.*" Do you believe that? If so, start praying like you do!

One big caveat I want to mention with this point—God is not a "name-it-and-claim-it" God. Going back to our last point of consideration, if you are asking for God to (and believing He will) provide you with a million dollars in your bank account tomorrow so you may retire early, move down to the beach, and live the rest of your years in laid-back luxury, do not be surprised when you check your account balance tomorrow and fail to see a significant deposit. Recall Jesus's words in John 14:13 (ESV): "Whatever you ask in my name, this I will do, that the Father may be glorified in the Son." God cares about answering your prayers, so others will see Him at work in your life (or theirs) and glorify His name.

George Müller wasn't praying for a smooth or quick ride free from the fog for his own sake, comfort, or convenience. Rather, I believe his petitions to lift the fog were made (and ultimately answered) so the captain of that ship—and future hearers of this story—could witness the awesome power of the One who controls the waves and the sea (Matthew 8:27), bringing glory and honor to God alone. (And probably also so George Müller could minister to the people in Quebec that Saturday.)

Keep a list of answered prayers. As I read that story about George Müller, I am left wondering how he exhibited that much faith in God to remove the fog and get him to his destination on time. Perhaps it could be related to the fact "Müller had over fifty thousand specific recorded answers to prayers in his journals, thirty thousand of which he said were answered the same day or the same hour he prayed them."[16] It reminds me of lyrics to the chorus of Elevation Worship's song *"Do It Again"*:

> I've seen You move, You move the mountains,
> And I believe I'll see You do it again,
> You made a way, where there was no way,
> And I believe I'll see You do it again.[17]

If you do not already have a system in place to record how God has answered your prayers, please start now. As God continues to answer prayers and my record of such grows, my confidence and faith in His ability to come through the next time I am in the midst of a storm are strengthened. Yours can too by taking this simple step.

Wait on God to answer your prayers. As a society, we have become known for desiring instant gratification. We become agitated when we don't get our order from a fast-food restaurant in less than five minutes, we start grumbling if we have to wait at a red light for more than 60 seconds, and we expect expedited responses to emails, phone calls, or text messages. Collectively, our motto best emulates the words of the rock group Queen, when they sang, "I want it all, and I want it now."[18] Unfortunately, that desire for immediacy is reflected in our prayer lives as well, where we often take matters into our own hands if God doesn't answer prayer in *our* timing.

David exhorts us in Psalm 27:14 (ESV) to "Wait for the LORD; be strong, and let your heart take courage; wait for the LORD!" We may think we will grow weary during our season of waiting, but in reality, "they who wait for the LORD shall renew their strength; they shall mount up with wings like eagles; they shall run and not be weary; they shall walk and not faint" (Isaiah 40:31, ESV).

Submit to God's omniscience. There are times we may be praying for an outcome that seems like an ideal result in the short term, but in the long run, such a result would do more harm than good. Take, for instance, a job opportunity in another town that would cause you to be further away from your aging parents. Your pursuit of that promotion is squashed, but a year later you find out your father has been diagnosed with terminal cancer and is going to need your help keeping up the maintenance of his home. In retrospect, if you had received that promotion, you would not have been able to care for him in the manner he needed during that time. The LORD declares in Isaiah 55:9 (NLT), "For just as the heavens are higher than the earth, so my ways are higher than your ways and my thoughts higher than your thoughts." There are times we cannot see the forest for the trees, but our All-knowing Father in Heaven—who is in the past, present, and future—sees it all. Submit to His knowledge and trust His ways, timing, and plans are better than anything you can imagine for your life.

We all walk through hard times. In those moments, it is tempting to ask merely for deliverance from the difficulty. Instead, I would encourage you to ask God through prayer, "What is Your purpose for me in this?" He may reveal that He is accomplishing His will through your trial to mature, to heal, or to cleanse some area of your heart. When your desire is for God's will to be done above all, the purpose He is achieving outweighs the pain of your circumstance.

As we close this chapter, consider these words from a few spiritual giants in the Christian faith who speak to the necessity, power, and purpose of prayer:

> "To be a Christian without prayer is no more possible than to be alive without breathing." - Martin Luther

> "The Christian life is not a constant high. I have my moments of deep discouragement. I have to go to God in prayer with tears in my eyes, and say, 'O God, forgive me,' or 'Help me.'" - Billy Graham

> "True prayer is neither a mere mental exercise nor a vocal performance. It is far deeper than that - it is spiritual transaction with the Creator of Heaven and Earth." - Charles Spurgeon

> "Is prayer your steering wheel or your spare tire?" - Corrie ten Boom

> "Prayer does not change God, but it changes him who prays."
> - Søren Kierkegaard[19]

Jesus's atoning death for our sins on the Cross made a way for you and me to commune directly with God in prayer (Matthew 27:51). That is not something I want to take for granted; do you?

Questions to Consider

1. Do you think you talk to God enough throughout your day? If not, what do you need to give up or change to do so?

2. How have you seen God answer your prayers in the past day? Week? Month? Year? As you think through these blessings from God, how has that strengthened your faith in Him?

EIGHT

Worship:
To Whom or What is Your Praise Directed?

When you think of the term *worship*, what immediately comes to mind? Is it songs you sing at church, or maybe your overall church experience on Sunday mornings? Merriam-Webster defines *worship* as the following: "to honor or revere as a divine being or supernatural power; to regard with great or extravagant respect, honor, or devotion."[20] J.I. Packer defines *worship* as "all of our direct communion with God: invocation, adoration, meditation, faith, praise, prayer and the receiving of instruction from his word, both in public and in private."[21] Patrick Morley suggests *worship* is "more than an event or activity—it's a lifestyle of submission to God."[22]

Why we worship

With those definitions in mind, you may be wondering why we should cultivate this particular spiritual discipline in our daily lives. I would offer you the following reasons for doing so.

God deserves our praise. Open your Bible and take a moment to read Psalm 146. As you do, meditate on some reasons God deserves our worship from this psalm alone. For instance, who else made the heavens and the earth? Who else provides for our every need? Who else saves us from hell? Who else heals us? Who else watches over us? No one but God. Recognition of these truths alone should cause us to bow down in worship and reverence to Him!

God commands it. In 1 Chronicles 16:7-36, David tells a group of priests how they ought to praise God. Here are some excerpts from that passage:

> Give praise to the LORD, proclaim his name; make known among the nations what he has done. Sing to him, sing praise to him; tell of all his wonderful acts…Sing to the LORD, all the earth; proclaim his salvation day after day. Declare his glory among the nations, his marvelous deeds among all peoples…Ascribe to the LORD the glory due his name; bring an offering and come before him. Worship the LORD in the splendor of his holiness. Tremble before him, all the earth!…Give thanks to the LORD, for he is good; his love endures forever (vv. 8-9, 23-24, 29-30a, 34, NIV).

Notice David was not making a recommendation for God's leaders to worship our Wonderful Creator—he was commanding them to do so. In Deuteronomy 6:13 (CSB; emphasis added), Moses directed the Israelites to "Fear the LORD your God, *worship him*, and take your oaths in his name," a command Jesus later reiterates in Luke 4:8. We take seriously God's commands to not steal, murder, or defame His holy name; why don't we take His command to worship Him as seriously?

God seeks it. Second Chronicles 16:9a (NIV) states, "the eyes of the LORD range throughout the earth to strengthen those whose hearts are fully committed to him." God is actively looking for you to commit yourself to Him, and the amazing thing is that He rewards you when you do! Why would you want to miss out on that blessing? Here is a convicting statement from Patrick Morley: "God is seeking worshippers. So if God and man don't get together, it's not because He's hiding—it's because we are. *We worship because we must*."[23] That latter, emphasized part of Morley's quote leads to the final reason for worshipping God.

We yearn for it. In 2005, coming off a third Super Bowl victory, star quarterback Tom Brady was interviewed by *60 Minutes* correspondent Steve Kroft. During the interview, Kroft asked Brady what he had learned about himself over the course of his successful career to date. Here was part of Brady's response: "Why do I have three Super Bowl rings, and still think there's something greater out there for me? I mean, maybe a lot of people would say, 'Hey man, this is what is.' I reached my goal, my dream, my life. Me, I think: God, it's gotta [*sic*] be more than this. I mean this can't be what it's all cracked up to be. I mean I've done it. I'm 27. And what else is there for me?"[24]

Wow. Here is a man who appears to have it all by the world's standards: fame, fortune, Super Bowl rings, and MVP trophies, but something is still missing in his heart. Unbeknownst to him, Brady mentioned what was missing in the interview—God. Blaise Pascal was once quoted as saying:

> This [man] tries in vain to fill with everything around him, seeking in things that are not there the help he cannot find in those that are, though none can help, since this infinite abyss can be filled only with an infinite and immutable object; in other words by God himself.[25]

Let us not look to anything or anyone else but God to fill that yearning, and in doing so, allow the words from Psalm 42:1 (NIV) to reign true in our lives: "As the deer pants for streams of water, so my soul pants for you, my God."

How to worship

So now that we have established why we ought to worship our Awesome God, let us unpack some practical ways to do so. A few years ago, Chris Tomlin and Darren Whitehead released a book entitled *Holy Roar*.[26] In it, they break down the seven Hebrew words that are translated into the English word *praise*, each of which represents a different aspect of what it means to truly praise and worship God. Read on for your daily Hebrew lesson:

1. yāḏâ: To revere or worship with extended hands; to hold out your hands.[27] Psalm 7:17 (NIV) is an example of this type of praise, when David writes, "I will give thanks to the LORD because of his righteousness; I will sing the praises of the name of the LORD Most High." If I can be fully transparent with you, prior to being introduced to this iteration of the word, I was hesitant to raise my hands in worship, rationalizing my unwillingness to do so by thinking, "That's just not who I am." And, to be honest, it isn't who I am—if I am inwardly focused on myself. All the more reason why I need to heed the words of Jesus in Luke 9:23, deny myself, and worship the God who has gifted me with eternal life in the manner He has said He wants me to!

2. hālal: To boast; to rave; to celebrate.[28] How many of us have overzealously celebrated our favorite team winning a big game? Or boasted to others about the size of the deer we recently shot? Are you willing to boast about and celebrate your Creator who knows every detail of your life (Psalm 139:1-6) in a similar manner?

3. zāmar: To make music; to give praise in song and music.[29] Psalm 98:5 (NLT) exhorts us to "Sing...praise to the LORD with the harp, with the harp and melodious song." When you sing songs of worship, are you truly praising our Almighty, Omnipotent, Sovereign God, or are you just going through the motions by merely reciting the words you see on a screen or in a hymnal?

4. tôḏâ: Thanksgiving; a sacrifice of praise.[30] Psalm 26:6b-7 (NLT) affirms we should "come to your altar, O LORD, singing a song of thanksgiving and telling of all your wonders." We discussed the concept of thanksgiving in our discussion on prayer earlier, but couldn't we all agree God has blessed us abundantly?

Don't just think materially, but in a spiritual and physical sense as well. Even in the worst circumstances, the breath we have is a gift from God. If you are reading this book, you know how to read, and that is something for which we can thank God. We ought to worship Him in thanksgiving for all He has done, is doing, and will continue to do in our lives!

5. bārak: To kneel; to bless God (as an act of adoration); to salute; to thank.[31] Psalm 95:6 (NIV) encourages us to "Come, let us bow down in worship, let us kneel before the LORD our Maker." In Luke 17:16 (NIV), shortly after being healed of leprosy, the cured man "threw Himself at Jesus' feet and thanked Him." When we kneel before our God in prayer, we visualize our surrender to His divine authority over our lives. Further, this humble act of worship acknowledges who we are in comparison to our Mighty God. One day, every knee will bow and every tongue will confess Jesus is Lord (Philippians 2:10-11); why not get in the practice of doing so now?

6. tᵊhillâ: A hymn; a song of praise; "praise (demanded by qualities or deeds or attributes of God)."[32] Whereas the Hebrew word *hālal* means to *speak* words of praise to our Heavenly Father, this version of the word means to *sing* songs of praise to God. I have little songs I sing to Amy when I get in a silly mood—about how much I adore her, love her, and think she's beautiful. This type of praise is similar, whereby we sing songs of praise to our Father out of an overflow of love, adoration, and appreciation in our heart for who He is and what He has done for us.

7. šāḇaḥ: To address in a loud tone; to shout; to commend, glory, and triumph.[33] When you worship, do you receive odd looks from those standing nearby, perhaps curious as to why there is so much noise coming from your mouth? Or, are you tamping down your enthusiasm for God out of fear of what others may think? If it's the former—and your motives are purely out of a desire to adore, thank, praise, and testify to God's goodness and faithfulness—then you are on the right track to biblical worship.

It may feel intimidating to consider what obedient worship to God looks like, but examples from Scripture encourage us that real men are willing to glorify God, regardless of the opinion of others. I think of David "leaping and dancing before the LORD" when the Ark of the Covenant was brought into Jerusalem and how Michal "despised him in her heart" when she saw his celebratory behavior (2 Samuel 6:16, NIV). When she questioned him regarding his behavior, David responded, "I will celebrate before the LORD. I will become even more undignified than this, and I will be humiliated in my own eyes" (2 Samuel 6:21b-22a, NIV).

Read also these convicting words from Ezra 3:10-13 (NIV; emphasis added):

> When the builders laid the foundation of the temple of the LORD, the priests in their vestments and with trumpets, and the Levites (the sons of Asaph) with cymbals, took their places to praise the LORD, as prescribed by David king of Israel. With praise and thanksgiving they sang to the LORD: "He is good; his love toward Israel endures forever." And all the people gave a great shout of praise to the LORD, because the foundation of the house of the LORD was laid. But many of the older priests and Levites and family heads, who had seen the former temple, wept aloud when they saw the foundation of this temple being laid, while many others shouted for joy. No one could distinguish the sound of the shouts of joy from the sound of weeping, because *the people made so much noise. And the sound was heard far away.*

Men, let us not concern ourselves with what others may think of us if all we talk about is God's goodness; or who may notice if our hands are raised high as we sing songs of praise to our Heavenly Father; or the looks we may receive if we humble ourselves in prayer by kneeling in the presence of a holy God. Instead, let us fix our eyes on "The LORD" who "alone deserves, all of the praise" (Psalm 115:1, CEV) and worship Him with all our heart.

Worshipping God with our body

In 1 Corinthians 6:19 (NIV), Paul asks the Corinthian church the following question: "Do you not know that your bodies are temples of the Holy Spirit, who is in you, whom you have received from God?" He goes on to command the Corinthians (and us) to "honor God with your bodies" in the next verse. So let's break down these two verses by first reminding ourselves of the construction of God's temple in the Old Testament. Great detail is found in Exodus 25 through 31 of God's instructions for the building of His tabernacle (or temporary/mobile temple), where He would dwell. First Kings 6 offers a glimpse into the more permanent fixture for God's dwelling, this time in the form of a temple. In both passages, we can draw the following conclusions about God's dwelling places:

- There were specific instructions on how to prepare and care for the tabernacle/temple;
- Only the finest materials were used to construct these structures; and
- God communicated with His people in both of these places.

Fast forward to the present, and recall those who have trusted in Jesus Christ as their Lord and Savior now have the Holy Spirit residing in them. In other words, as Paul explains in 1 Corinthians 6:19, God—in the form of the Holy Spirit—now dwells in you, which makes your body a temple for God. So skim right back up to the three conclusions we drew from those Old Testament passages and consider the following about your own body:

- Are you taking considerable care to preserve God's temple?
- Are you "constructing" your temple with the finest materials?
- Are you sensing God communicating with and through you?

These are important questions to ponder when we consider Jesus's response to those who were using God's temple for selfish gain in Matthew 21:12-13 (ESV): "Jesus entered the temple and drove out all who sold and bought in the temple, and he overturned the tables of the money-changers and the seats of those who sold pigeons. He said to them, 'It is written, 'My house shall be called a house of prayer,' but you make it a den of robbers.'" If Jesus expressed righteous anger with those utilizing His temple for fleshly gain, don't you think He has something to say about how we are using our temples (i.e., bodies) for selfish gain as well?

You may be curious as to how you are to honor and worship God with your body, so allow me to suggest to you a few ways in which you may do so.

Exercise. I can already hear the excuses mounting: "I don't have time to exercise," "I don't have anywhere I can exercise," "I can't afford a gym membership," or perhaps "I just don't feel like exercising early in the morning or after a long day of work." I get it. Because I have made the same excuses for why I cannot honor and worship God in this manner. The truth, though, is that you can set aside something your flesh would prefer to do (e.g., watching TV, scrolling mindlessly through social media) to cultivate this discipline. Honestly, with all the advances in technology, you could exercise while watching TV or looking at social media on your phone at the same time! Discard the other excuses about logistics, because you can exercise at home in your living room, on your street, up and down your apartment stairs, or wherever else you can find a conducive spot. Gyms and their memberships could be attractive "sprinkles" on your exercise "cupcake," but they are not necessities to get you started.

Now, to the final excuse I mentioned—and if we are honest with ourselves, all other excuses revolve around this one—being "disinclined to activity or exertion,"[34] which is a friendly way of referring to our own laziness. So let's look at some Scriptural references regarding the term *laziness* to see how God views this state of mind:

"Laziness casts one into a deep sleep, and a lazy man will suffer hunger" (Proverbs 19:15, NASB).

"The soul of the sluggard craves and gets nothing, while the soul of the diligent is richly supplied" (Proverbs 13:4, ESV).

"Whoever is slothful will not roast his game, but the diligent man will get precious wealth" (Proverbs 12:27, ESV).

"Through sloth the roof sinks in, and through indolence the house leaks" (Ecclesiastes 10:18, ESV).

Reading through these verses convinces me God does not care for our propensity for laziness. Although that alone motivates me to get off the couch and onto the treadmill, I want to share another motivator that has resonated with me lately. Research abounds relating to the many health benefits of exercise. Specifically, just 30 minutes of physical exertion a day can lead to better heart health, weight loss, stress reduction, higher energy, improved memory, and enhanced productivity.[35] As a husband and a father, I want to be my best self for my family for however long God has purposed me to be on this earth, and to do so, I have resolved to make sacrifices now that will honor God with my body (Romans 12:1). Whatever ministry God has called you to, being able to fulfill it well involves stewarding the physical body He has given you.

Marinate on this thought for a moment—if you saw your local church was overgrown with weeds, needed a paint job to enhance its image, or could use some new seating to replace the worn-out upholstery, you probably would not bat an eye to assist with those efforts. So why should we approach our bodies (as temples of God) any differently when we have a few weeds, dents, or fabric tears around our waistline? Remember, this is not about a vain attempt to look good or attract attention, but rather about taking care of your body so you can do the things God is calling you to.

Eat well. You have just come out of the deer stand. It was a cold, rainy day, and your journey back to the truck resulted in accumulating mud all over your boots. On your way back home, you remember you need to swing by the church to pick up a sippy cup that your daughter left in her Sunday School room. Do you change your shoes before entering the church office? Chances are, you do it without thinking twice, as you do not want to pollute a structure symbolizing God's dwelling place. Yet oftentimes—and I am talking to myself here—we do not think twice about putting something into our body that is detrimental to the place where the Holy Spirit resides. Listen, I am probably the biggest consumer of sweets I know, but we have to be more mindful of the long-term effects of what we eat. Read God's take on this:

> "Be not among drunkards or among gluttonous eaters of meat, for the drunkard and the glutton will come to poverty, and slumber will clothe them with rags" (Proverbs 23:20-21, ESV).

> "If you have found honey, eat only enough for you, lest you have your fill of it and vomit it" (Proverbs 25:16, ESV).

> "For, as I have often told you before and now tell you again even with tears, *many live as enemies of the cross of Christ.* Their destiny is destruction, *their god is their stomach,* and their glory is in their shame. Their mind is set on earthly things" (Philippians 3:18-19, NIV; emphasis added).

The Hebrew word for *gluttonous* in Proverbs 23:20 can be translated as one who is a riotous or vile eater.[36] Are you eating the whole carton of ice cream in one sitting or just a bowl? The answer to that question could very well determine whether your stomach is your god and thus, whether your destiny is destruction (Philippians 3:19).

Sabbath. In the book of Genesis, we read the account of God creating the heavens, the earth, and all living creatures (including humans) inhabiting His creation. For six days, God worked, but "By the seventh day God had finished the work he had been doing; so on the seventh day he rested from all his work. Then God blessed the seventh day and made it holy because on it he rested from all the work of creating that he had done" (Genesis 2:2-3, NIV). I bring this up to assert that if our Creator saw fit to rest from His work, why do we neglect to do so? I am convinced we have simply become too busy by engulfing ourselves in our careers, hobbies, and/or children's activities to find time to rest.

I want to encourage you to go back for a moment to God's identification of the seventh day—He referred to it as *holy*. The Hebrew word for *holy* here means to be consecrated, dedicated, or set apart.[37] Interestingly, it is from the same word used for *holy* in Leviticus 11:45b (NIV), when God commanded the Israelites to "be holy, because I am holy." God takes this concept so seriously that—in the Ten Commandments—He instructed us to set aside one day a week to rest. Read the following excerpt from that passage: "Remember the Sabbath day by keeping it holy. Six days you shall labor and do all your work, but the seventh day is a Sabbath to the LORD your God. *On it you shall not do any work*" (Exodus 20:8-10a, NIV; emphasis added).

Now, unless you have a pretty sweet gig, chances are you work five days a week. Like most of us, you have a list of chores or activities to tend to on one of your off days. Which leaves one other day for rest—theoretically. Yet, again, as a society, we have let other things impede upon this day that is to be set apart to the LORD, instead replacing it with temporary things (e.g., work, tasks around the house, hobbies, sporting events) that carry no eternal significance and provide no margin for rest. We can rationalize our behavior by saying, "I am trying to be an invested father by attending all of my son's baseball games" or "I am ministering to a lost person in a deer stand" or "I need to be available when my clients need me." We have already discussed how the devil tries to manipulate what you believe to be true with his lies, so I would just challenge you to think about the last time you truly rested (and I'm not just talking about your sleep at night). When is the last time you turned off the notifications on your phone, switched off the TV, set down the computer, put up the paint brush, and just rested?

I am not going to dive into the theological interpretations of how long your Sabbath should be, when you should take your Sabbath, or what you should do during your Sabbath. What I would remind you of is this—we make time for what is important to us. And if something is important to God (as all His commands are), it ought to be important to a man of God as well.

Keep yourself pure. If I can be fully transparent with you, I used to enjoy watching a lot of television, and quite honestly, the vast majority of what I watched would not be considered wholesome entertainment. I also used to spend a lot of idle time scrolling through my phone—either on the internet or on social media applications. In retrospect, my time spent on these mindless activities was not productive in the least. Then God convicted me one Sunday while I was teaching high school boys about keeping themselves pure, and He did so by using Paul's words in Philippians 4:8 (NASB) as the conviction mechanism. Here, Paul concludes his letter to the Philippian church by encouraging readers to dwell (i.e., meditate, savor, camp out) on "whatever is true, whatever is honorable, whatever is right, whatever is pure, whatever is lovely, whatever is commendable." As I was reading these words to those teenage boys, I felt God's rebuke and correction. That afternoon, I went home and deleted the TV shows saved on the DVR, as well as removed my social media accounts that did not lend themselves to pure, lovely, and honorable thoughts.

You may think, "What is the big deal if I have a guilty pleasure here and there?" Well, let's go back to the Bible for our answer to that question. James tells us in the latter part of James 1:27 (ESV) that we are to keep ourselves "unstained from the world." Think with me for a moment about a glass of water—pure and clean, undefiled by the outside world. But then you decide to put one small drop of red food coloring in that glass, and all of a sudden, all of the water turns red. One drop pollutes the whole glass, as you cannot extract the food coloring once it has been dropped into the water. That is EXACTLY what happens when we let impure images and words into our minds, hearts, eyes, and ears. We cannot unsee what we see or unhear what we hear. You may think you can compartmentalize those worldly influences, but I know from my own experience that my behavior is different when I am savoring those secular thoughts over the things Paul encourages me to dwell on in Philippians 4:8. As pastor Johnny Hunt says, the devil just wants one acre of your 100-acre plot, because he knows if he can access one acre, more acres will surely follow.[38] That is a sobering thought, but one that is so true.

I challenge you to do some introspection here. What do you need to give up to be "all-in" for God? Is it something you are watching? Is it something you are listening to? Is it a website you like to frequent? Is it a conversation you like to have (or perhaps a person with whom you like to converse)? Only you can answer that, but I cannot appeal to you enough that there is no way you can straddle the fence with one foot in God's yard and one foot in the world's (i.e., the devil's). One foot in the world means both feet are in opposition to God. As James says, "You adulterous people! Do you not know that friendship with the world is enmity with God? Therefore *whoever wishes to be a friend of the world makes himself an enemy of God*" (James 4:4, ESV; emphasis added).

Before we move on, I want to take a moment to convince you that you are capable of biblical worship. Have you ever attended a live sporting event? Perhaps one of your children's games or that of your favorite professional or college team? If you have, you know the environment surrounding those games—one of anticipation, excitement, enjoyment (most of the time), and the thrill of victory. You also know how many people react to certain situations by joining the crowd with shouts of praise toward their team, cheers for a job well done, and songs attributed to those teams or players.

I want to ask you a few probing questions as it relates to your behavior at these sporting events: 1) have you ever exuded all your heart, soul, mind, and strength at a game, and 2) are you worn out after watching your favorite team play? Here is how God convicted me several years ago as it related to my favorite college football team. I was so quick to raise my hands, to cheer, to shout, to scream, to sing (fight songs), and to boast during and after games, but then when I went to church on Sunday mornings, I was a statue. Moreover, among men, I was so quick to talk about how my team was faring, but rarely did I broach the subject of what God was doing in my life. I felt like God was asking me, "Would others say you worshipped Me or your football team more?" Listen—sporting events, teams, and players let us down, but our God never does! Sporting events, teams, and players do not provide for our every need, but our God does! Sporting events, teams, and players do not save us from the pit of hell, but our God does! It may not be sports that get you riled up, but if we are honest with ourselves, we all have our golden calves that threaten to take the place of worshipping God (Exodus 32).

Here's the deal—we know what it means to rejoice, we know what it means to raise our hands in praise, we know what it means to shout, and we know what it means to act with thanksgiving and joy. Furthermore, we know how to fill our bodies (including our minds) with substance and information. So the main question to consider is this: to whom or what is our worship directed? Remember, God commands that we "shall have no other gods before [Him]" (Exodus 20:3, NIV); can that be said of you? He wants and deserves all the glory, honor, and praise (Revelation 4:11; Psalm 145:3), but when our focus is inward, the only ones receiving glory and praise are ourselves. I implore you to humble and deny yourself, lift up your eyes to the King of kings and Lord of lords, and worship the only One who saves (Psalm 68:20)!

Questions to Consider

1. What gets in the way of you wholeheartedly worshipping God?

2. What specific changes do you need to make to improve your worship experience—in song, in word, and within your body?

NINE

Faith:
Our God Never Fails

Merriam-Webster defines *faith* as "complete trust; belief and trust in and loyalty to God."[39] The author of Hebrews states, "faith is confidence in what we hope for and assurance about what we do not see" (Hebrews 11:1, NIV). In his commentary on the book of Hebrews, R. Kent Hughes suggests *faith* can best be described as "a solid conviction resting on God's words that make the future present and the invisible seen. Faith has as its core a massive sense of certainty."[40] As we will see in a familiar Old Testament story, "godly faith is really 'trust.' What we have seen of God's nature and character should lead us to trust Him, and trust naturally leads to obedience."[41]

Consider with me the following account of faith (and lack of faith) in action. In Numbers 13, the LORD instructed Moses to send a group of men to explore the land of Canaan (i.e., the Promised Land). Moses chose one leader from each of the 12 Israelite tribes to fulfill the LORD's command. These men were tasked with a reconnaissance mission—seeking to determine the lay of the land. Among their directives was to "See what the land is like and whether the people who live there are strong or weak, few or many. What kind of land do they live in? Is it good or bad? What kind of towns do they live in? Are they unwalled or fortified? How is the soil? Is it fertile or poor? Are there trees in it or not?" (Numbers 13:18-20a, NIV). In essence, the Israelites were relying on these 12 men to plot out their operational strategy for commandeering the land God had promised to give them. What follows was their report back:

They came back to Moses and Aaron and the whole Israelite community at Kadesh in the Desert of Paran. There they reported to them and to the whole assembly and showed them the fruit of the land. They gave Moses this account: "We went into the land to which you sent us, and it does flow with milk and honey! Here is its fruit. But the people who live there are powerful, and the cities are fortified and very large. We even saw descendants of Anak there. The Amalekites live in the Negev; the Hittites, Jebusites and Amorites live in the hill country; and the Canaanites live near the sea and along the Jordan" (Numbers 13:26-29, NIV).

On the surface, this report may not seem too alarming, but digging deeper, we notice a tremendous lack of faith in God within this debrief to the Israelites. Here is why: in Genesis 12:1-3 (ESV), God told Abraham, "Go from your country and your kindred and your father's house to the land that I will show you. And I will make of you a great nation, and I will bless you and make your name great, so that you will be a blessing. I will bless those who bless you, and him who dishonors you I will curse, and in you all the families of the earth shall be blessed." This promise to make Abraham and his descendants into a great nation was later affirmed to Moses in Exodus 3:17 (ESV). Here, God declared to Moses, "I will bring you up out of the affliction of Egypt to the land of the Canaanites, the Hittites, the Amorites, the Perizzites, the Hivites, and the Jebusites, a land flowing with milk and honey." If you have spent time reading through Exodus, you will remember God *did* deliver the Israelites from the Egyptians through a multitude of plagues and also by drying up a 7,254-foot-deep body of water—the Red Sea. You may also recall that once the Israelites crossed over the Red Sea, the parted waters rescinded, engulfing, overwhelming, and killing their Egyptian enemies (Exodus 14).

I articulate all of this for you because I want to now go back to Numbers 13, specifically to the report received from those who were commissioned to scope out the Promised Land. Notice the following from verses 27 and 28 (NIV; emphasis added): "We went into the land to which you sent us, and it does flow with milk and honey! Here is its fruit. *But the people who live there are powerful, and the cities are fortified and very large. We even saw descendants of Anak there."* These leaders recognized the land flowed with milk and honey (just as God said in Exodus 3:17), but they also noticed something else—fearsome opponents (the Hebrew word for *Anak* in verse 28 is translated into "giant"[42]). So, yes, the Promised Land was just as God had described, but in order to take control of it, some big people were going to have to be defeated.

Now to his credit, Caleb—one of the 12 chosen to survey the land—added onto the summary of the land in Numbers 13:30b (NIV), stating the Israelites still "should go up and take possession of the land, for we can certainly do it." Yet poor Caleb was quickly silenced by the majority of his fellow explorers who kept their eyes on the giants, comparing their own stature to "grasshoppers" among their enemies to further dissuade God's people from trying to enter into the Promised Land (Numbers 13:30-33).

Numbers 14 begins with more grumbling among the Israelite camp, which has now hitched their wagon to those who were afraid of the inhabitants of Canaan. Their fear was so strong that many desired to go back to Egypt where they were once slaves. (Let this be a lesson in the power of your words, by the way!) That was until one of the 12 surveyors of the Promised Land—Joshua—stepped in to silence the doubters. Let's read his account from Numbers 14:7-9 (NIV; emphasis added): "The land we passed through and explored is exceedingly good. If the LORD is pleased with us, he will lead us into that land, a land flowing with milk and honey, and will give it to us. Only do not rebel against the LORD. And *do not be afraid of the people of the land, because we will devour them. Their protection is gone, but the LORD is with us. Do not be afraid of them.*"

How was Joshua able to exhibit such faith in God? Keep in mind he had experienced God delivering the Israelites from the yoke of slavery in Egypt, where God displayed His wonderful, mighty, miraculous power in a number of ways. From that personal encounter, Joshua had an intimate knowledge of who God was and what He was capable of doing. Seeing God orchestrate the circumstances surrounding the Israelites' exodus from Egypt strengthened Joshua's faith. As a result, the next time he experienced a seemingly insurmountable situation (descendants of Anak), he would be resolute in his confidence in God to do exactly what He said He would do (bring the Israelites into the Promised Land). Notice the contrast between Joshua and 10 of the other tribal heads (remember, Caleb—the 12th surveyor of the land—encouraged the Israelites to press forward as Joshua did). The ten leaders encouraging the Israelites to retreat fixed their eyes on their circumstances, and their faith in God subsequently wavered. Joshua kept his eyes focused on who God was, what He had done before, and what He promised He would do. Subsequently, his faith endured.

Here is one more thing to consider about Joshua's admirable faith. Not only did he and the Israelites face the prospect of battling against giants, but they also faced another impossible obstacle in the form of crossing another body of water—the Jordan River—to enter the land promised to them by God. Joshua 3:13-17 (NIV) recaps the journey:

> "And as soon as the priests who carry the ark of the LORD—the Lord of all the earth—set foot in the Jordan, its waters flowing downstream will be cut off and stand up in a heap." So when the people broke camp to cross the Jordan, the priests carrying the ark of the covenant went ahead of them. Now the Jordan is at flood stage all during harvest. Yet as soon as the priests who carried the ark reached the Jordan and their feet touched the water's edge, the water from upstream stopped flowing. It piled up in a heap a great distance away, at a town called Adam in the vicinity of Zarethan, while the water flowing down to the Sea of the Arabah (that is, the Dead Sea) was completely cut off. So the people

crossed over opposite Jericho. The priests who carried the ark of the covenant of the LORD stopped in the middle of the Jordan and stood on dry ground, while all Israel passed by until the whole nation had completed the crossing on dry ground.

Notice the progression here:

- **God made a promise to His people through Joshua.**

"And as soon as the priests who carry the ark of the LORD—the Lord of all the earth—set foot in the Jordan, its waters flowing downstream will be cut off and stand up in a heap" (Joshua 3:13, NIV).

- **His people encountered an impossible obstacle.** (Henry Blackaby refers to this as a *crisis of faith*[43])

Now the Jordan is at flood stage all during harvest (Joshua 3:15a, NIV).

- **His people trusted God, believed His promises, and moved forward in faith.**

Yet as soon as the priests who carried the ark reached the Jordan and *their feet touched the water's edge* (Joshua 3:15b, NIV; emphasis added).

- **His people saw God's mighty power and experienced His promises fulfilled.**

[T]he water from upstream stopped flowing…while all Israel passed by until the whole nation had completed the crossing on dry ground (Joshua 3:16-17, NIV; emphasis added).

I hope you caught what I was trying to convey here. Yes, God gave the Israelites a promise, but notice He did not dry up the Jordan River *until* His people responded in faith. Then, *as soon as* His people showed their trust in God by stepping into the banks of a flooding river, God dried up the overflowing body of water.

God delivered His people in a miraculous manner, not so the Israelites could boast about how they had navigated these mighty waters in their own strength. Instead, He performed this magnificent act so "all the peoples of the earth might know that the hand of the LORD is powerful and so that you might always fear the LORD your God" (Joshua 4:24, NIV). God—not you or me—is the hero of our life and the ONLY One who deserves praise and glory (2 Corinthians 10:17). By the way, if you read on in the book of Joshua, you will see Joshua led the Israelites into the Promised Land, as God yet again did exactly what He said He would do.

Word of warning

As you read about having faith in God to help overcome the figurative giants in your life, I do want to caution you against believing one of the devil's lies. Do not assume—just because you are trusting God or following the steps outlined above—He will necessarily grant you *temporary* victory or reprieve over the storm, the illness, the circumstance, the person, the you-fill-in-the-blank you are facing. There are times when God has a purpose for allowing affliction to remain. I think of the story of Hagar, who was despised by her mistress (Sarah) for conceiving a son with Abraham (which, ironically, was Sarah's idea). Sarah was not at all kind to Hagar, mistreating her to the point where Hagar fled from her mistress. Yet "the angel of the LORD told her, 'Go back to your mistress and submit to her.'" (Genesis 16:9, NIV). God saw Hagar's affliction and sent her right back into the tumultuous situation.

I think also of our Lord and Savior Jesus Christ. Knowing full well the persecution to come upon Him through betrayal, arrest, and violent death, Jesus prayed, "'Father, if you are willing, take this cup from me; yet not my will, but yours be done.' An angel from heaven appeared to him and strengthened him" (Luke 22:42-43, NIV). We know God did not remove Jesus from the events that followed (and praise God that He didn't), but did you catch the last part of that passage? After Jesus submitted His will to His Father's, God strengthened and equipped Jesus to go through the impending storm.

There may be times when God wants to take you right through a storm, so that when the next one buffets, your personal experience with Him will give you courage. However, even if God never takes you out of your trial, and the situation you are facing ends in earthly death, praise God for a Savior who has secured for you an eternal place in Heaven with Him!

Faith in action

So how do we get to the point where we are exhibiting the type of faith Jesus modeled for us on the evening of His betrayal? How do we obtain the type of faith that will help us face the giants, impossible circumstances, or obstacles on the horizon? Is it possible to secure the type of faith that trusts in God in the midst of the storm—regardless of whether He intends to deliver you from it? Quite simply, that type of faith is obtainable, but it only comes through knowing God more intimately. (And who knew God more intimately than His Son, as Jesus says in John 10:30?). At the risk of sounding like a broken record, your knowledge of God grows by cultivating the spiritual disciplines we have been unpacking over the past few chapters. Let me give you a tangible example of what I mean.

In October 2018, Hurricane Michael was quickly approaching the Florida Panhandle, and just north of that, the city in which we live. The morning this category five= storm was set to make landfall, I had to make a decision: should we stay in our home or evacuate to Amy's family in Birmingham, which was safe out of the path of destruction? Further convoluting my thought process was the fact our oldest son was just six months old at the time, so any extended time without power would not be ideal. And with over 20 towering, mature oak and pine trees on our property, an extended loss of power appeared imminent.

I began that day just like I do every day—in God's Word and in prayer. As I began to pray for protection over our home, I felt like God—through His Holy Spirit—was telling me to be still and quiet. (Remember one of those suggestions I gave you in the chapter on prayer?) It was then the Holy Spirit brought to mind a familiar passage in Mark 4:35-41 (CSB):

> On that day, when evening had come, he told them, "Let's cross over to the other side of the sea." So they left the crowd and took him along since he was in the boat. And other boats were with him. A great windstorm arose, and the waves were breaking over the boat, so that the boat was already being swamped. He was in the stern, sleeping on the cushion. So they woke him up and said to him, "Teacher! Don't you care that we're going to die?"
> He got up, rebuked the wind, and said to the sea, "Silence! Be still!" The wind ceased, and there was a great calm. Then he said to them, "Why are you afraid? Do you still have no faith?"
> And they were terrified and asked one another, "Who then is this? Even the wind and the sea obey him!"

As soon as I read those words, I felt a tremendous peace fall upon me. God reminded me that He had the power to calm the storms and still the winds, and through His Holy Spirit, had given me a promise that He would protect us and our home. With that assurance in mind, I decided for us to hunker down and ride out the storm. The decision to have faith in God during that crisis was an easy one for a couple of reasons. First, God had given me other promises before and proven Himself faithful. This knowledge of who God had shown Himself to be in prior circumstances strengthened my faith in Him as we faced this fast-approaching hurricane. (As an aside, I just want to remind you that being able to look back on how God has proven Himself faithful with a record of answered prayers is so critical to a growing faith.) Second, I knew God's character was One that does not change (Malachi 3:6). "So," I thought, "if God proved Himself faithful to me before, He would unequivocally do so again." As the hurricane passed through our area with winds over 100 miles per hour, the trees swayed and branches fell, but while countless others not more than two miles from our home had trees fall through their roofs and lost power for a week, we lost power for all of five hours without one tree uprooted. All praise and glory to our Mighty God and Protector!!

Take note, though, I would not have been able to experience this sort of faith if I was not spending time in His Word—having knowledge of His character and that passage in Mark 4 that He led me to—and presenting my requests and anxieties to Him in prayer. You see, our ability to exhibit a strong, sincere faith comes through knowing and experiencing Him, and knowing and experiencing Him is dependent upon us reading His Word, offering up our prayers and petitions to Him, and worshipping Him with all of our heart, soul, mind, and strength on an ongoing, consistent basis.

One more note about this story. I believe if God knew trees were going to fall on our home, He could have spoken differently—a word of warning—in which case obedience would have looked like evacuating. Or if He told me to stay, and a tree fell on our home, that He would have had a plan and purpose in that as well. When our highest priority is obeying God for the sake of His glory, we cannot lose.

As I close, I want to provide you with a list of some things I put my faith in today: that my car would operate properly, that the heaters would keep our home warm during sub-freezing temperatures, that the milk would not be spoiled since the date on the carton had not yet passed, and that the workers in the drive-thru restaurant would get my order correct. For each of these moments of my day, I did not give any thought to the outcomes, because, *more often than not*, all of these things come to fruition without incident.

Notice I said, "more often than not," which implies there are times where these outcomes result in frustration, angst, or illness, as none of them perform perfectly day in and day out. Yet, unless the negative outcomes become more consistent, I still do not hesitate to put my full confidence, trust, and faith in them. Do you know there is Someone who never fails us? Recapping the deliverance of the Israelites into the Promised Land, Joshua reminds us that "None of the good promises the LORD had made to the house of Israel failed. Everything was fulfilled" (Joshua 21:45, CSB). God promises to never leave us or forsake us (Deuteronomy 31:6; Joshua 1:9), and since He is the same God today as He was over 2,000 years ago when making that promise to His people, we can have faith and trust in Him to do for us *exactly* what He says He will do. That—unlike a car, appliance, beverage, or restaurant worker—is Someone worth trusting and having full confidence in!

Questions to Consider

1. Is something holding you back from having complete trust in God? If so, what is it?

2. In what ways has God proven Himself faithful to you?

PART THREE

Foundational Functions

"We are therefore Christ's ambassadors, as though God were making his appeal through us. We implore you on Christ's behalf: Be reconciled to God" (2 Corinthians 5:20, NIV).

TEN

Spiritual Leadership:
Christ's Ambassadors

John Maxwell defines leadership as "influence, nothing more, nothing less."[44] As Christian men, I would submit we possess a certain degree of influence—whether knowingly or unknowingly—among those around us. However, I fear many men have not taken the time to fully comprehend what it means to be a spiritual leader in all aspects of their lives. So before we jump into our specific functions for foundational manhood, I would like to take some time to share with you this broader role of spiritual leadership that encompasses all of our other responsibilities. Specifically, there are several qualities we should possess to effectively lead in our homes, our communities, and our workplaces.

Purpose-driven. Paul proclaims in 2 Corinthians 5:20 (NIV; emphasis added), *"We are therefore Christ's ambassadors*, as though God were making his appeal through us. We implore you on Christ's behalf: Be reconciled to God." Merriam-Webster defines the term *ambassador* as "an authorized representative or messenger" or "a diplomatic agent of the highest rank."[45] As foundational men, we are to serve as spiritual leaders within our spheres of influence; however, do not ever forget that God Almighty is THE Spiritual Leader of our lives. Because of this truth, we are to submit our plans and purposes to His will. As Christ's ambassadors, our purpose and the message we are to share are made clear by Jesus in Matthew 28:19-20a (NIV), when He tells His disciples to "go and make disciples of all nations, baptizing them in the name of the Father and of the Son and of the Holy Spirit, and teaching them to obey everything I have commanded you."

Taking Jesus's command into account, our dual-focused mission toward those God has entrusted into our care is to 1) ensure they are aware of God's message of love, grace, mercy, redemption, and reconciliation (i.e., sharing the Gospel) and once saved, 2) help them navigate their new spiritual journey with their Savior (i.e., discipleship). As I have mentioned before, fulfilling this mission to the sons God blessed us with was a huge impetus behind me completing this book. So I want you to consider your own spheres of influence—do you need to share the good news of Jesus atoning for the sins of the world with someone you know? Or, do you need to encourage a fellow believer to deny himself and submit to God's authority, leadership, and transforming power in his life? If the answer is "yes" to either or both of these questions, I pray you will have the courage to begin those conversations.

Noble character. Paul encourages his mentee Timothy to "set an example for the believers in speech, in conduct, in love, in faith and in purity" (1 Timothy 4:12b, NIV). Is your example worthy of following? In 1 Timothy 3, Paul provides for us a list of character qualities that should be present in overseers of the church, and as spiritual leaders, we can extend this application to our spheres of influence (i.e., home, workplace). This is a set of traits that should be identifiable not only in pastors but in all Godly men:

> Now the overseer is to be above reproach, faithful to his wife, temperate, self-controlled, respectable, hospitable, able to teach, not given to drunkenness, not violent but gentle, not quarrelsome, not a lover of money. He must manage his own family well and see that his children obey him, and he must do so in a manner worthy of full respect...He must also have a good reputation with outsiders, so that he will not fall into disgrace and into the devil's trap (1 Timothy 3:2-4, 7, NIV).

Gifted evangelist and Bible teacher Francis Dixon condensed these verses into a list of traits defining noble character. Below are a few of his musings; take note of how many qualities are reflected in your personality:

1. A man who is above reproach
2. A man of unquestioned moral integrity
3. A man of Christian grace and spiritual discipline
4. A man who is generous-hearted and hospitable
5. A man who is able to teach
6. A man with a right attitude to money
7. A man who manages his own family well
8. A man who is spiritually taught and mature[46]

Billy Graham once said, "When character is lost, all is lost."[47] Warren Buffet is quoted as saying, "It takes 20 years to build a reputation and five minutes to ruin it."[48] Right or wrong, there is a target on our backs as Christian leaders. People enjoy pouncing on the failures of others, particularly among a group the world thinks is supposed to be perfect. (Ironically, our failures are exactly why we are Christians; we need a Savior to save us from our sins!) In this age of social media, news can travel across the world and be seen by millions of people in a matter of seconds. We must allow the Holy Spirit to manifest in us character traits similar to those Paul outlines in the aforementioned passage, as to not give the devil or a watching world an opportunity to diminish our effectiveness as spiritual leaders.

Humility. In Proverbs 22:4a (HSCB), Solomon says, "The result of humility is fear of the LORD." He states in Proverbs 8:13a (NIV), "To fear the LORD is to hate evil." Are you tracking with me? Some of you may be familiar with transitive law. If not, let me give you a brief synopsis: if A equals B and B equals C, then A equals C.[49] In this case then, humility (A)—defined as "freedom from pride or arrogance"[50]—results in hating evil (C). So when we humble and deny ourselves (Luke 9:23), we grow to hate evil and despise sin, just as

God does. Conversely, when we think of ourselves more (and pride prevails), we do not have the same disdain for evil. Since our flesh is rooted in sin, when we think of ourselves more than we ought, evil is bound to be a natural overflow. Consider some more pitfalls of pride, as well as some benefits to humility:

> "When pride comes, then comes disgrace, but with humility comes wisdom" (Proverbs 11:2, NIV).

> "Pride brings a person low, but the lowly in spirit gain honor" (Proverbs 29:23, NIV).

> "Pride leads to destruction; humility leads to honor" (Proverbs 18:12, CEV).

Three separate verses in Proverbs—God's book of wisdom—articulate the following consequences of pride: disgrace, being humbled, and destruction. Alternatively, those who are humble gain wealth (not necessarily financial), wisdom, and honor (Proverbs 22:4). Which side do you want to be on?

Here are some other benefits of humility that will make you a more effective spiritual leader. First, possessing humility allows us to admit wrongs and apologize for them. Prideful leaders think they can do no wrong, while humble leaders acknowledge their errors and ask for forgiveness from those they have hurt. Humble leaders are also willing to ask for help, counsel, and advice when needed, yet those who are consumed with themselves think they have all the answers. Humble leaders share with others in the decision-making process, while individuals with selfish, impure motives are not willing to share control on any matter. Finally, humble leaders are willing to kneel on a dirty floor to wash the feet of those they lead, similar to how Jesus washed His disciples' feet (John 13:1-20). However, those rooted in pride have their own feet out in anticipation of others washing them.

Spiritual Leadership: Christ's Ambassadors 105

As Christ's ambassadors, we would do well to model our lives after Jesus, "who, though he was in the form of God, did not count equality with God a thing to be grasped, but emptied himself, by taking the form of a servant, being born in the likeness of men. And being found in human form, he humbled himself by becoming obedient to the point of death, even death on a cross" (Philippians 2:6-8, ESV).

Servant. I am always fascinated to read differing theories on the topic of leadership—particularly as it relates to servant leadership. Robert K. Greenleaf published an essay in 1970 with the following ideas on this topic:

> The servant-leader is servant first… It begins with the natural feeling that one wants to serve, to serve first. Then conscious choice brings one to aspire to lead. That person is sharply different from one who is leader first, perhaps because of the need to assuage an unusual power drive or to acquire material possessions…The leader-first and the servant-first are two extreme types…The difference manifests itself in the care taken by the servant-first to *make sure that other people's highest priority needs are being served.* The best test, and difficult to administer, is: *Do those served grow as persons? Do they, while being served, become healthier, wiser, freer, more autonomous, more likely themselves to become servants?* And, *what is the effect on the least privileged in society? Will they benefit or at least not be further deprived?*…*The servant-leader shares power, puts the needs of others first and helps people develop and perform as highly as possible.*[51]

Reread those sentences above where I took the liberty to emphasize. Now compare those with the words of Jesus:

> Jesus called them together and said, "You know that the rulers of the Gentiles lord it over them, and their high officials exercise authority over them. Not so with you. Instead, *whoever wants to become great among you must be your servant*, and whoever wants to be first must be your slave—just as the *Son of Man did not come to be served, but to serve,* and

to give his life as a ransom for many" (Matthew 20:25-28, NIV; emphasis added).

Compare also Greenleaf's qualities associated with servant leadership with Paul's exhortation to the church at Philippi:

> Do nothing from selfish ambition or conceit, but in humility *count others more significant than yourselves*. Let each of you *look not only to his own interests, but also to the interests of others*. Have this mind among yourselves, which is yours in Christ Jesus (Philippians 2:3-5, ESV; emphasis added).

After meeting with Marine Corps Lieutenant General George Flynn, author Simon Sinek wrote a *New York Times* best seller entitled *Leaders Eat Last*. Describing the premise of the text, Sinek concluded, "Great leaders sacrifice their own comfort—even their own survival—for the good of those in their care."[52] Almost 2,000 years ago, the greatest Servant Leader of all—Jesus Christ—sacrificed His comfort for the good of those in His care. We who have the Holy Spirit dwelling inside of us have the mind of Christ (1 Corinthians 2:16), capable of following Jesus's example. As such, let us rise to the call to lead by laying down our lives for our wife, children, families, friends, neighbors, colleagues, and whomever else God has entrusted to us (John 15:13).

Courageous. For me, one of the most comforting and reassuring passages in the Bible comes from Joshua 1. After taking over for a spiritual giant (Moses), Joshua is tasked with leading the Israelites into the Promised Land. Before beginning his leadership role, I cannot help but think Joshua may have been facing doubts regarding his ability to take over leading God's people in place of a legend like Moses. I make this assumption because we see God command Joshua to "be strong and courageous" three separate times over the span of nine verses in

Joshua 1, and two other times in this same passage God reassures Joshua that He will be with him wherever he goes (Joshua 1:1-9, NIV).

God knows we cannot fearfully lead those He has entrusted to our care, so to subvert this type of thinking, He gives us a promise that He will be with us wherever we go (Joshua 1:9). We must move forward in faith with this promise, clinging to others from God's Word as well:

> "Even though I walk through the darkest valley, I will fear no evil, for you are with me; your rod and your staff, they comfort me" (Psalm 23:4, NIV).

> "Then they cried to the LORD in their trouble, and he saved them from their distress. He sent out his word and healed them; he rescued them from the grave" (Psalm 107:19-20, NIV).

From my experience leading and watching others lead, I can tell you those in our spheres of influence gain confidence from our courage. Alternatively, these same individuals start to lose hope when we lose ours. Jesus Christ never wavered in His courageous journey to and on the Cross. We more than likely will not face the same plight He did, so what is stopping us from showing just an ounce of His courage to those we lead and serve?

Effective Communicator. Solomon states in Proverbs 18:21a (NIV), "The tongue has the power of life and death." Those we are responsible for leading lean on us to provide them with encouragement, reassurance, comfort, and guidance—just like the disciples did with Jesus. Proverbs 25:11 (CSB) affirms, "A word spoken at the right time is like gold apples in silver settings." Consider what type of fruit you are dishing up for those closest to you: harmful, hateful, or spiteful words that destroy a person, or words that build up, provide direction, embolden, equip, encourage, and bring life to a soul? As Christ's ambassadors, we ought to ensure our words are "full of grace [and] seasoned with salt" (Colossians 4:6, NIV), not letting "any unwholesome talk come out of [our] mouths, but only what is helpful for building others up according to their needs, that it may benefit those who listen" (Ephesians 4:29, NIV). Salt, by the way, adds flavor (i.e., life) and prevents decay (i.e., death).

As effective communicators, not only is the use of our words of paramount importance (and influence), but how we use our ears to listen to others should be of the utmost consideration as well. As men, we tend to want to solve problems. So when a spouse, child, friend, or colleague comes to us with an issue, we often interject with how we would solve the problem if we were in their shoes. Granted, these interruptions are often well-intentioned, but there are times those around us just want an ear to listen. James 1:19 (NIV) reminds us to "be quick to listen, slow to speak." There is an old Irish Proverb that states, "God gave us two ears and one mouth, so we ought to listen twice as much as we speak."[53] I am not going to put a word counter and timer on you and be legalistic about your word-to-listening ratio, but I would challenge you to ask others how good of a listener you are. If the answer is not the most flattering, I pray their response will spur you on to enhance this critical element of effective communication.

Protector. We tend to apply the idea of a protector to husbands and dads—and we are. However, Jesus exemplifies this characteristic in a broader role as a spiritual leader. In John 17, Jesus prayed for His disciples—those of whom Jesus said to God "you gave them to me" (John 17:6b, NIV)—then for all those to come who would believe in Him (John 17:20-26). Specifically, these two statements from Jesus jump out to me:

> "While I was with [the disciples], I *protected* them and kept them safe by that name you gave me" (John 17:12a, NIV; emphasis added).

> "My prayer is not that you take them out of the world but that you *protect* them from the evil one" (John 17:15, NIV; emphasis added).

As I reflect upon this example of Jesus protecting and praying for His disciples, here are some questions I now ask myself as a protector to those whom God has entrusted to me:

- What are my wife and kids watching or listening to?
- Where are my wife and kids hanging out?
- With whom are my wife and kids hanging out?
- What will my children be taught in school?
- Is my family spending time and living in a safe and secure environment?
- Do those I lead at work know I support, care, and appreciate them?
- Do I know the needs of those I am leading?

You may think some of these questions are a bit overbearing, perhaps even controlling, but when you are before God and giving an account for all He has entrusted to you (Romans 14:12), would you rather be on the side of being too protective or too careless? I'll choose the former every day, no matter what people may think of me.

Eternally-focused. I have often heard it said, "this world will drag you down if you let it." As I look across our nation, I see much truth in this statement. As I write this, our country is in the midst of battling the Coronavirus pandemic, which has killed close to two million people worldwide over the past 12 months. Debates are ongoing about who was the rightful winner of the recent Presidential election, a suicide bomber just orchestrated a terrorist attack in the heart of Nashville, and the unemployment rate is slowly making its way down from peaking at 14.7%—the highest it has been since the Great Depression.[54] Suicide and divorce rates are increasing,[55] church attendance is dwindling,[56] and racial hostility seems to be getting worse by the day.

Closer to home, you may have been laid off from your job recently, worrying about how you are going to put food on the table for your children. You or your spouse may have just been dealt a bleak health diagnosis, or you may have just been stabbed in the back by a close friend or co-worker. Any or all of these circumstances may drag you down if your perspective is not properly focused, but I want to encourage another lens from which to view life's circumstances. This wisdom comes from Paul in 2 Corinthians 4:

> We are hard pressed on every side, but not crushed; perplexed, but not in despair; persecuted, but not abandoned; struck down, but not destroyed…Therefore we do not lose heart. Though outwardly we are wasting away, yet inwardly we are being renewed day by day. For our light and momentary troubles are achieving for us an eternal glory that far outweighs them all. So *we fix our eyes not on what is seen, but on what is unseen, since what is seen is temporary, but what is unseen is eternal* (vv. 8-9, 16-18, NIV; emphasis added).

When our eyes are fixed on temporary matters (e.g., worry, fear, loss of life), we lose heart quickly and begin to sink. However, when we keep our eyes fixed upon eternity, we are freed to fulfill God's call to lead those He has entrusted to our care.

As spiritual leaders, we are called to courageously lead, protect, and communicate to those in our spheres of influence with a focused purpose, noble character, humble spirit, servant's heart, and eternal mindset. It is a tall task, but one that is possible if we are willing to yield ourselves to God and allow Him to manifest His fruit in our lives.

I often tell the student-athletes I work with that they represent the image of our school to the public—particularly when they wear their athletic gear out in the community. Their actions—whether positive or negative—affect the way people view our institution. As Christians, we are always wearing a ball cap with "JC" on the front and a uniform inscribed with "Jesus" across our chests. As an ambassador of our Savior, how well are you representing Him and His interests to those around you? The answer to that question will undoubtedly affect your ability to lead effectively as we review the forthcoming roles and responsibilities of a Christian man.

Questions to Consider

1. Are those within your sphere of influence able to see Jesus Christ through your words and actions? If there is room for improvement, in what ways do you need to deny yourself to become a more effective ambassador for Christ?

2. Where are you looking out for your own interests above those of others?

3. Are you effectively attending to, taking care of, and guarding those God has entrusted to you?

ELEVEN

Husband:
Prophet, Priest, and King

According to the American Psychological Association, approximately 40 to 50 percent of marriages end in divorce.[57] Research from the American Academy of Matrimonial Lawyers indicates the number of millennials (18-to-34-year-olds) seeking prenuptial agreements continues to rise.[58] Findings from a recent study suggest that almost half of Americans believe that open relationships are morally acceptable. Of those responding to the survey, 64 percent of women believe open relationships are immoral, while only 47 percent of men feel that way.[59] Suffice it to say, our nation and men, in particular, are not taking the concept of marriage as seriously as God intended.

For a glimpse into His intentions for marriage, we need to look no further than Genesis 2:24 (NIV), where the Word of God says, "a man leaves his father and mother and is united to his wife, and they become one flesh." My wife was teaching to a group of high school girls one Sunday morning, and she illustrated this concept of two becoming one flesh to them. (She borrowed the example from Pastor Chris Hodges.) She took two pieces of construction paper and glued them together; then after a few minutes, she tried to separate the two pieces of paper. Not surprisingly, pieces of each remained attached to the other. It brings to mind Jesus's response to the Pharisees on the topic of marriage and divorce, when He said, "what God has joined together, let no one separate" (Matthew 19:6b, NIV).

For more insight into God's design for marriage, let us turn our attention to Ephesians 5. Here, Paul states, "the husband is the head of the wife as Christ is the head of the church, his body, of which he is the Savior." (v. 23, NIV). A couple of verses later, Paul commands husbands to "love your wives, just as Christ loved the church and gave himself up for her" (Ephesians 5:25, NIV). Here we see a comparison drawn where the husband is to Christ as the wife is to the church. Later in Scripture, we read: "Let us rejoice and be glad and give the glory to Him, for the marriage of the Lamb has come, and His bride has prepared herself" (Revelation 19:7, NASB). The Lamb referred to in this verse is Jesus, and His bride is the church (i.e., Christians).

Piecing these verses—Genesis 2:24, Ephesians 5:25, and Revelation 19:7—together, we can draw a parallel between the type of relationship Christ has with His church and what He intends for us in marriage. When you say, "I do," God intends for that to be a lifelong covenant bond—just like Jesus's covenant with you when you accepted Him as your Savior (John 10:28)—not an "I'll stay committed as long as I feel like it" relationship. As alluded to earlier, many couples enter into marriage without a proper perspective of God's view on marriage. As a result, at the first sign of opposition, one of the spouses opts out, claiming they "no longer love their spouse" or "they have found someone else who meets their needs."

Granted, both marriage partners have a responsibility to seek God diligently, but as the spiritual leaders of our homes, men must make a resolute commitment to fight daily for our marriages, because there is an enemy who actively seeks to divide our homes and conquer our lives. With that in mind, I would like us to look at guidance and instruction from God's Word on a husband's foundational functions, roles, and responsibilities in marriage, and to do so, we will look further at Paul's words to married couples in Ephesians 5:

> Wives, submit yourselves to your own husbands as you do to the Lord. For the husband is the head of the wife as Christ is the head of the church, his body, of which he is the Savior. Now as the church submits to Christ, so also wives should submit to their husbands in everything.

Husbands, love your wives, just as Christ loved the church and gave himself up for her to make her holy, cleansing her by the washing with water through the word, and to present her to himself as a radiant church, without stain or wrinkle or any other blemish, but holy and blameless. In this same way, husbands ought to love their wives as their own bodies. He who loves his wife loves himself. After all, no one ever hated their own body, but they feed and care for their body, just as Christ does the church—for we are members of his body. "For this reason a man will leave his father and mother and be united to his wife, and the two will become one flesh" (vv. 22-31, NIV).

Prophet, priest, and king

This instruction for husbands to "love your wives, just as Christ loved the church and gave himself up for her to make her holy, cleansing her by the washing with water through the word, and to present her to himself as a radiant church, without stain or wrinkle or any other blemish, but holy and blameless" (Ephesians 5:25-27, NIV) has a lot of meat to chew on, so I hope you brought your appetite. First, we need to understand our primary role in marriage is to show Jesus Christ to our bride. Our motive in doing so is not to make her fall more in love with us, but rather so she may fall more deeply in love with her Savior. Borrowing some wisdom from Patrick Morley's *Man in the Mirror*,[60] I would like to offer three roles Jesus—as the loving Groom—perfectly displays for husbands to imitate.

Prophet. I want us to explore two aspects of a husband's role as a prophet: 1) speaking for God and 2) representing God to his bride.

1. A prophet speaks for God. In the Old Testament, God used men of faith (e.g., Jeremiah, Isaiah, Joel, Hosea, and Ezekiel) to convey messages to His people. Some of these messages were hopeful, while others called for the audience to repent and turn from their wicked behavior. Similarly, God used Jesus to share a message of hope and repentance to a lost, fallen world (John 3:16-17). So I ask you: how well are you conveying God's message of hope and repentance to your wife?

Go back to Ephesians 5 for a moment, where Paul says men are to present their wives "without stain or wrinkle or any other blemish, but holy and blameless" (v. 27, NIV). Are you—as a mouthpiece for God—encouraging your wife's spiritual growth? How about insisting on church attendance and corporate worship? Have you offered to watch the kids or pick up one of the household chores to allow her to do a Bible study at church? More fundamentally, does your wife own a Bible? Have you considered leading a devotion for just the two of you? Do you pray with her daily, ask her about her time with God, and inquire about how God is speaking to her? Speaking of prayer, although close to half of the marriages in the United States end in divorce, less than one percent of married couples who pray together daily end up separating.[61] I implore you to consider what you are doing to help your spouse grow more and more into the image of Christ. Yes, everyone is responsible for their own spiritual growth, but we, as husbands, can certainly create an environment that fosters our wife's sanctification.

2. A prophet represents God to his bride. Our only hope for fulfilling this second aspect of a husband's role as a prophet is allowing the Holy Spirit to work in us. Read this discourse between Jesus and Philip, one of His disciples:

> Philip said, "Lord, show us the Father and that will be enough for us."
> Jesus answered: "Don't you know me, Philip, even after I have been among you such a long time? *Anyone who has seen me has seen the Father.* How can you say, 'Show us the Father'? Don't you believe that I am in the Father, and that the Father is in me? The words I say to you I do not speak on my own authority. Rather, *it is the Father, living in me, who is doing his work*" (John 14:8-10, NIV; emphasis added).

As you think about representing our Heavenly Father to your wife, I would ask you to consider the following—are your actions toward her defined as pure, considerate, accommodating, merciful, sincere, peaceful, patient, kind, faithful and self-controlled? Or, are your behaviors more along the lines of impure, conflict-ridden, harsh, cold-hearted, manipulative, hateful, impatient, mean-spirited, untrusting, and brash? Recall, the former qualities are some of the 17 qualities Christ modeled during His earthly ministry, while the latter is indicative of a man who is controlled by his own fleshly, sinful desires.

Finally, representing God to our spouse ought to consist of the same type of love He has toward us. The Greek word for *love* found in John 3:16 signifies an unconditional form of love that is not based on anything the recipient does.[62] Practically speaking, this means your love for your bride is not predicated on her ability to keep the house clean, fix your favorite meal, or fulfill your sexual desires—you would love her even if none of those needs were met. Can that be said of the love you have for your wife?

Priest. Whereas a prophet represents God to people, a priest represents people to God. Hebrews 5:1 (NIV) affirms this point: "Every high priest is selected from among the people and is appointed to represent the people in matters related to God." As our Great High Priest (Hebrews 4:14), Jesus 1) prayed for those entrusted to His care (John 17:6-26) and 2) sacrificed Himself for the atonement of our sins (1 John 2:2). As husbands who are emulating an earthly shadow of this role, we are to serve as mediators to God on behalf of our spouse, as well as be willing to sacrifice ourselves for the sake of our bride.

1. A priest prays for his wife. Our priestly responsibility ought to consist of spending time in prayer for our wife—remembering her needs, concerns, and anxieties. Ask God to speak to her during her time in His Word and in prayer, and if there are any areas in which she needs to repent, that God would bring about conviction. Spend time praying for God to equip her for each moment of the day and for each "hat" she wears (e.g., daughter, teacher, mentor, mentee, accountability partner, wife, mother, helper, friend). Pray also for unity in mind, body, and spirit as it relates to your marriage and that the enemy will have no foothold in your lives—individually and as a couple. I also encourage you to pray for her protection—spiritually, physically, emotionally, and mentally. Pray her body is used for God's glory alone and that He would grant her wisdom to make decisions that bring Him honor. In essence, cover her whole body—inside and out—in intercessory prayer.

2. A priest sacrifices himself for the sake of his bride. In this role as priests, we are also to go so far as to lay down our lives (i.e., deny ourselves) for our spouses. When is the last time you let her sit on the couch and relax while you did the dishes? When did you last give up an opportunity to go fishing or hunting with your friends so your wife could go get a pedicure? Can you think of a time when you focused on meeting her needs in the bedroom at the expense of your own?

One day, I made a concerted effort to deny every selfish inclination I had, instead opting to sacrifice my desires for the sake of serving my bride. By the end of the day—because I had to be so intentional about my actions and attitude, and because my wife does so much on a daily basis around the house with our kids—I was mentally and physically exhausted, wondering how I could possibly do this daily. But then God reminded me of the Great High Priest, who willingly sacrificed His divine privileges in Heaven (Philippians 2:7) and suffered a cruel death to atone for my sins. If I am to love my wife as Christ loved (and continues to love) me, one day of sacrificial behavior was just the beginning, and thankfully I have the Holy Spirit equipping me to do what God expects of me (Philippians 2:13).

King. "Wives, submit yourselves to your own husbands as you do to the Lord. For the husband is the head of the wife as Christ is the head of the church, his body, of which he is the Savior. Now as the church submits to Christ, so also *wives should submit to their husbands in everything*" (Ephesians 5:22-24, NIV; emphasis added). Now men, before you rush over to your wife, open your Bible to Ephesians, read this passage to her, and demand she respect and follow your leadership, I want to dispel a couple of myths about these verses. First, this passage does not mean you rule your marriage. You may ask, "But didn't Paul just say I am the head of my wife?" Yes, he did. But did you keep reading to see that Christ is the head of the church (which includes you)? So yes, husbands are spiritual leaders in the home, but God is still THE leader in the home. Wives are to submit to their husbands, but husbands are still accountable and responsible to God. Do not ever misinterpret these verses to mean you are the supreme leader, thus making no room for God—whether intentionally or unintentionally.

Secondly, these verses do not suggest the wife has no voice in the marriage relationship. Paul does say that wives are to submit to their husbands in everything, but we would be wise to glean some knowledge from Proverbs as it relates to seeking (and ignoring) input from others:

> "Surely you need guidance to wage war, and *victory is won through many advisers*" (24:6, NIV; emphasis added).

> "For lack of guidance a nation falls, but *victory is won through many advisers*" (11:14, NIV; emphasis added).

> "*Plans fail for lack of counsel*, but with many advisers they succeed" (15:22, NIV; emphasis added).

When God created woman in Genesis 2, He did so because He noticed "It is not good that the man should be alone," so He made "a helper fit for him" (v. 18, ESV). God knew husbands needed a companion—a helpmate from whom we would receive assistance and wisdom. Men, your wife is there to help you, not just cook all of your meals and do all of the household chores. Accept God's intended role for your spouse by asking for, seeking, and using her wise counsel.

So now that we have established what Paul's instruction to wives does not mean, we can turn our focus to what this passage suggests about a husband's role as a king. We have already discussed a great deal about spiritual leadership within our spheres of influence, but as it specifically relates to our roles as husbands, there are three more responsibilities we should add to our list. Specifically, when I consider the earthly ministry of the King of kings—Jesus Christ—I think of One who 1) knew and is known by His bride, 2) provided for His bride's needs and welfare, and 3) acted in a manner worthy of receiving honor.

1. A king knows and is known by his bride. Here is my conviction: if I am going to effectively lead my wife, I need to know her, and she needs to know me. Jesus says in John 10:14b (NIV), "I know my sheep and my sheep know me." The Greek word for *know* used here is *ginōskō*, which is synonymous with the "Jewish idiom for sexual intercourse between a man and a woman."[63] Obviously, then, when we say we are to *know* our spouse, we are not talking about surface-level knowledge like her favorite food, color, or flower. We are referring to deep, intimate knowledge, on par with what you may discover about your bride during romantic encounters where you are fully exposed—*nothing* is hidden.

Quite simply, we should know everything about our wife and she should know everything about us. The latter may be more difficult for us as men because we do not like to convey our fears, weaknesses, and doubts to anyone else. However, if we are to truly become one flesh, a spirit of openness between both spouses needs to be cultivated. Discover her love language. (If you haven't read Gary Chapman's *5 Love*

Languages, do yourself a favor, earn some brownie points, and suggest you and your wife read this together.) Make time to discuss your high and low points of the day. Let her be the first one you run to when you have great or sobering news, and set goals for your marriage together. In our role as king, we ought to know every detail of our wife—just as God knows the number of hairs on our head (Luke 12:7). Knowledge of our wives will help us better lead and pray for them, as we know where they are weak, vulnerable, and in need of support.

2. A king provides for his wife's needs and welfare. In Paul's exhortation to husbands in Ephesians 5:28-30 (NIV; emphasis added), he advocates for husbands "to love their wives as their own bodies. He who loves his wife loves himself. After all, no one ever hated their own body, but they *feed and care for their body, just as Christ does the church*—for we are members of his body." In Matthew Henry's commentary on how Jesus fed and cared for His bride (i.e., the church), he states Jesus "furnishes with all things that he sees needful or good for her, with whatever conduces to her…welfare."[64]

Recount just a few of the numerous miracles Jesus performed, as outlined in the Gospels: the feeding of the 5,000 (Matthew 14:13-21), turning water into wine (John 2:1-12), healing a blind man (John 9:1-12), casting out an unclean spirit (Mark 1:21-28), and raising Lazarus from the dead (John 11:38-44). In the book of Revelation, we see Jesus fighting on behalf of His bride and defeating the enemy of our souls—the devil. In Revelation 1:18b (NIV), we read an affirmative declaration from Jesus that—by holding "the keys of death and Hades"—He has conquered the grave, so those who believe in Him could do the same (John 3:16). In each of these instances, Jesus's heart was focused on providing for His bride's needs and welfare.

So as husbands, how should we go about fulfilling this facet of kingship? First, let me clearly state God is our Ultimate Provider, not us. Even still, we have a role to play here, too. I would submit just a few tangible examples to help you get started. To begin, once you determine your spouse's love language, speak it, and speak it often. Nothing can be more disheartening to a woman than for her to know her husband is aware of what would make her feel loved, valued, appreciated, and needed, then have those needs ignored. Next, ensure she feels safe and secure in your home and with those living around you. For instance, does she feel comfortable playing with the kids outside or jogging in your neighborhood, or is she reluctant to step foot outside your home?

Lastly, work diligently so that—if at all possible—your wife does not feel obligated to work outside the home. Some women long to be stay-at-home wives so they can better serve their husbands and/or children. Be willing to take on a part-time job (so long as the extra time away does not mitigate your ability to meet her other needs) to make this a priority. Talk together about what you two might be able to give up, if needed, to make this happen. For example, my wife says she would rather be home raising our children on a day-to-day basis than to have a vehicle if it came down to it. And she gladly forfeits fancy trips or expensive clothes that a job outside the home might allow for. I can testify your marriage will be strengthened if your wife at least has this as an option on the table. This is a hang-up for a lot of men; I get it. Money allows us to buy things. But most of our families need less stuff and more time.

These are just a few practical ways we, as kings, can meet our wives' needs to promote their welfare. However, I would encourage you to have a candid conversation with your wife to discover specific ways she feels her spiritual, physical, and emotional needs are not being met, then take steps to improve your behavior. You may say, "Well what about her? She sure doesn't meet my needs." Keep in mind that God did not wait for us to clean up our act before showing His love to us by sending Jesus to die for our sins (Romans 5:8). I would implore you, therefore, to not fear being the one in your relationship who loves the most—just like our King has done and continues to do with us.

3. A king acts in a manner worthy of receiving honor. When I think of the position of a king, I think of royalty, prestige, respect, and honor. Certainly, when I think of King Jesus, these images of grandeur are amplified. As kings to our brides, we, too, ought to live in a manner worthy of receiving honor. Martin Luther once said of husbands, "let him make her sorry to see him leave."[65] Is this how your wife feels when you leave for work in the morning? If not, I challenge you to dive deep into the disciplines we have discussed, drawing near to God and allowing Him to make Himself known, present, and visible in your life (James 4:8). Only when we start disciplining our minds to replace old attitudes, thoughts, and desires with new ones (Ephesians 4:17-32) will our wife start to see the type of noble character on display we discussed at length in previous chapters.

I would also submit—not only do we need to behave in a manner worthy of honor and respect—we ought to bestow that same respect, dignity, and honor upon our wives. Jesus says in Matthew 7:12 (ESV), "whatever you wish that others would do to you, do also to them." When is the last time you praised your wife to her face or in front of others? When is the last time you opened her car door for her? How often do you thank her for a home-cooked meal? As men, we so desperately desire affirmation from others, but how many times have you told your wife you love her, are proud of her, think she is a good mom, and are so thankful to God for her in the past week?

God showed me something interesting in Proverbs 31 during my time in His Word recently. We often think of that chapter as a picture of the ideal wife, but in verses 28 and 29 (NIV; emphasis added), the Bible says, "Her children arise and call her blessed; *her husband also, and he praises her*: 'Many women do noble things, but you surpass them all.'" Even if you discover your wife's predominant love language is something other than words of affirmation, I assure you that you cannot go wrong in showering her with sincere words of gratitude, appreciation, and affection.

Prophet. Priest. King. Shepherding our wife as Jesus shepherds us. Loving our bride as Christ loves His church. Please do not become discouraged at the seemingly impossible mountain to climb. Remember, "God is working in you, giving you the desire and the power to do what pleases him" (Philippians 2:13, NLT). As we have addressed several times now, it is not in our strength, but that of the Holy Spirit working in us that helps us achieve God's will for us as husbands. And when that occurs, what a beautiful witness your marriage will be to others who see your relationship and get a glimpse of the glorious Gospel!

Questions to Consider

1. What practical ways can you show the love of Christ to your wife?

2. What is your wife's love language? If you do not know it, take time to identify it.

TWELVE

Husbands, Recapture Your First Love!

Do you remember what it was like when you and your wife were dating? Long walks on the beach, spending a great deal of time conversing with one another, you doing your best to impress her through gentlemanly acts of kindness, and presenting yourself as clean and hygienic (most of the time). Then suddenly, after you said "I do," those behaviors you employed to win her over slowly fade into oblivion.

Note these words from Revelation 2:2-5a (CSB; emphasis added): "I know your works, your labor, and your endurance, and that you cannot tolerate evil people. You have tested those who call themselves apostles and are not, and you have found them to be liars. I know that you have persevered and endured hardships for the sake of my name, and you have not grown weary. *But I have this against you: You have abandoned the love you had at first. Remember then how far you have fallen; repent, and do the works you did at first.*" In this context, God is referring to the love for Him that the church of Ephesus had. God is reminding His church we are to never come out of the honeymoon phase with Him, instead always possessing a similar attitude of elation, reverence, and appreciation for Him and what He has done for us—which subsequently leads to a deeper love for Him. Similarly, God never intended for us to distance ourselves from the honeymoon phase of marriage. Instead, He wants us to remain—and grow—in the fullness of love and adoration that we shared with our spouse together at the marriage altar.

Despite this expectation from God, many married couples allow the devil (in the form of the "daily grind") to chip away at the newlywed state of mind, slowly removing the passionate feelings one spouse shares for another. Before we realize what is going on, we view our spouse as nothing more than a roommate. Further illustrating this point, one study found that 75 percent of individuals seeking a divorce cited "lack of commitment" (i.e., fell out of love) as a major reason for seeking separation.[66] To those spouses, I would counter their faulty rationale with wisdom I once read: "our choices must lead and our feelings will follow."[67] Men, if you have found yourself abandoning the love you had for your wife at first, *choose* to acknowledge your wrongdoing, ask for forgiveness from God and your bride, and take specific steps to reclaim the honeymoon phase when you could not bear the thought of being apart from your wife for one second. What follows are a few action items (choices) to help you get started.

Date nights. Throughout the week, my wife and I are pulled in many different directions—work and raising little children will do that to you. By the time we get them in bed for the night, both of us are exhausted, leaving little time for quality fellowship with one another. So we have made it a priority to weekly let the boys go to their grandparents and grab dinner out. During this precious time, we are able to reconnect, catch each other up on anything we did not communicate during the week, and keep our relationship lively. If you do not have the luxury of built-in babysitters or access to anyone to watch the kids, do not use this as an excuse. Delay your dinnertime one night, put the kids to bed early, grab some takeout, and bring your date night to your kitchen table. Recapturing the love you had at first starts with doing some of the things you did—like going on dates—when you first fell in love with your wife.

Getaways. One of the best pieces of advice I received in our pre-marriage counseling was to take my bride on a getaway every six months. Admittedly, I initially questioned how I was going to pay for such a recommendation, but then the pastor who married us clarified that these trips do not have to be to all-inclusive destinations halfway across the world. Instead, he suggested I could make a reservation at a local hotel in town, whisking my wife to a special dinner and evening away from home. The impetus behind this suggestion was to get my wife and me out of the ordinary routine of day-to-day responsibilities and to reconnect as husband and wife. Except for the season in which I am writing (in the midst of a worldwide pandemic), we have held to this practice, and I can testify it helps keep our marriage in the newly-wed phase and out of the ditches.

House filled with joy. Budget-conscious and prudent husbands will appreciate this option, as implementing this recommendation will not cost you a dime. I have fond memories from my high school days of being in the home of a married couple that was always full of fun, joy, and laughter. Although this couple had been married for twenty years, it seemed like they were just as smitten with each other as the day they met.

I encourage you to take a moment to gauge the temperature in your home—is it one full of joy and laughter or stress and angst? If it's the latter, I want to remind you of Proverbs 17:22 (CSB), which states, "A joyful heart is good medicine, but a broken spirit dries up the bones." If you wonder why your marriage is drying up, consider the following quote from Dr. Tony Evans. In his book *Kingdom Marriage*, Evans says "husbands are the spiritual thermostats of their marriages and families, setting the spiritual temperature of the home. The wife, however, is the thermometer, indicating the actual temperature reading in the home."[68] Make certain the thermostat is on a setting that reads joy, fun, and laughter, and through your actions (e.g., implementing game nights or family dance parties), you'll soon find that the thermometer (your wife) is reading the same temperature.

Reigniting the flame. Before we move on to a few other pertinent issues in our marriages, I want to remind you of the original context of the verses from Revelation 2 that I shared with you just a moment ago. The church in Ephesus was doing some great works (e.g., did not tolerate evil, patiently endured hardships in Jesus's name), but they had drifted from their love for Him. As a result, God condemned their sin and commanded them to repent. Likewise, in your marriage relationship, you may find yourself implementing some of these aforementioned practical examples to help restore the tight bond you and your wife once shared. However, if you are not also acknowledging how you may have potentially wandered from your love for God, your work to enhance your marriage will be meaningless. Heed Jesus's words in Revelation 2, turn back to God by incorporating the disciplines we have unpacked so far, find yourself falling deeper in love with your Heavenly Father, and watch your marriage blossom!

Romance

If you jumped to this section anticipating a quick fix to enhance your sex life, I would caution you to tap the brakes a bit. I need you to know, our role in having a vibrant sex life is much bigger than just showing up in the bedroom. Specifically, the more emotionally connected your bride feels with you (often through your own sharing and vulnerability), the more attracted she will be to you. Do not buy into the devil's lie that sex is only a physical encounter—it goes much deeper than that.

To discover the deeper beauty of marital romance, let's start with some wisdom from God's Word to see what He has to say on this topic:

> The husband should fulfill his marital duty to his wife, and likewise the wife to her husband. The wife does not have authority over her own body but yields it to her husband. In the same way, the husband does not have authority over his own body but yields it to his wife. Do not deprive each other except perhaps by mutual consent and for a time, so that you may devote yourselves to prayer. Then come together again so that Satan will

not tempt you because of your lack of self-control (1 Corinthians 7:3-5, NIV).

Sex was intended for husband and wife. Paul starts this discourse by stating each spouse should "fulfill [their] marital duty" to one another. The English Standard Version of 1 Corinthians 7:3 refers to *marital duty* as "conjugal rights," also known as "the sexual rights or privileges implied by and involved in the marriage relationship."[69] God designed sex for man and woman to enjoy after—not before—wedding vows were shared. In the Old Testament, we see further evidence of this: man meets woman, they get married, then the "conjugal act" consummates the marriage covenant (Genesis 24:67; Genesis 29:21, for example).

To further illustrate this point, note the way God designed a woman's body. When a virgin woman first has sex with a man, her hymen breaks, which causes her to bleed.[70] This shedding of blood—intended to complete the marriage covenant—is analogous to Jesus's shedding of blood on the Cross to seal the marriage covenant between Himself and the church (His bride). As you can see, God takes sex very seriously and sacredly. So should we.

You do not own your body. The second thing I want you to see is you do not own your body. Because of that, we need to be willing to yield our sexual needs to hers. Practically speaking, this means you ensure she is satisfied before you concern yourself with your own satisfaction. Please understand, too, your bride may not be aroused as quickly as you, so be willing to patiently tend to the needs of your spouse. The same man writing 1 Corinthians—Paul—also wrote the book of Philippians, which, if you recall, included the appeal for us to look out for the interests of others above our own (Philippians 2:4). This exhortation does not stop when the lights go out.

I would also mention here that—just because the wife is to yield authority of her body to her husband—this does not mean we can or should ask her to do anything she is uncomfortable with (and certainly not anything counter to God's Word). Don't misinterpret or misuse God's Word just so you can have some flesh-created fantasy fulfilled at your wife's expense.

Do not deprive one another. In the aforementioned passage from 1 Corinthians 7, we see Paul's understanding of man's sexual drive—and consequently, one of the devil's easiest ways to make us stumble—when he acknowledges our lack of self-control in this area. Think of it this way. You come home after a long day of work and there is a huge five-course meal on the table. By the time you get to dessert, you don't think you have any room for another bite, but you keep eating out of respect for the time it took your wife to prepare this lavish feast. Upon completing the meal, your need for nourishment has been met and you do not want to even think about food again for several hours. Now, contrast that scenario with one where you come home and find a peanut butter and jelly sandwich on the table. After scarfing down those few bites, your mind is quickly jumping to what else you can find to eat because your physiological need for sustenance has not been met. Likewise, working together with your wife to cultivate a robust and fulfilling intimate life will leave you both satisfied and uninterested in pursuing extramarital pleasures.

A word on sexual immorality

In 2014, the porn industry made over $97 billion, with over $10 billion of that revenue coming from the United States.[71] Recent research found 43 percent of men have viewed pornography in the past week.[72] "According to the American Association for Marriage and Family Therapy, national surveys indicate…25 percent of married men have had extramarital affairs. The incidence is about 20 percent higher when emotional and sexual relationships without intercourse are included."[73] The data is right there in front of us—men struggle with sexual immorality.

I am convinced so many Christian men battle with this issue because they have bought into the devil's lie that lusting after a woman is not a big deal. "After all," the enemy whispers, "one look won't hurt anyone." Let me first counter that lie with truth from the Bible. Jesus says in Matthew 5:28 (NIV), "I tell you that anyone who looks at a woman lustfully has already committed adultery with her in his heart." There is no debate with Jesus. If you look lustfully at another woman—which means you desire to be sexually intimate with her—you have already committed the sexually immoral act of adultery and sinned against God. In His eyes, the actual act of sexual immorality often starts with "just a look."

Although God's Word stands on its own merit, I would like to also offer you some practical suggestions to help you overcome these cunning and deceitful overtures from the devil.

Pray. I tell men often how tough it is to sin while also talking to God simultaneously—in the same way you would find it difficult to cheat on your wife while talking to her at the same time. If you begin to pray for a way out of this temptation and find it difficult to articulate the right words, simply say, "Jesus, Jesus, Jesus," and the devil will flee at the sound of His mighty name (James 4:7).

Flee. You may recall the story of Joseph and Potiphar's wife in Genesis 39. Potiphar's wife persistently tried to seduce Joseph, to the point of physically grabbing him by the cloak and trying to pull him into the bedroom. Joseph jolted out so quickly that Potiphar's wife was left with Joseph's cloak in her hand, which she used to falsely accuse him. Even though he was imprisoned, Joseph was innocent before God because he did not spend time trying to talk his way out of temptation, instead darting out the door the moment danger reared its head.

Avoid idleness. In 2 Samuel 11, we read about David sending his men off to war, yet not going to battle himself as kings customarily did. As a result, he found himself bored and lonely one evening, and in his boredom, wandered up to the roof of his palace where he noticed a beautiful woman (Bathsheba) bathing across the way. The downward spiral of sexual immorality quickly commenced, with David facing a slew of long-term consequences for his sinful behavior (2 Samuel 12). However, if David had been off at war and keeping himself actively engaged in his leadership role as king, there would have been no time for lustful looks. So, if you find yourself idle, instead of picking up the phone, surfing the Internet on your computer, or tuning to a premium channel on your television, make better use of your time by calling an accountability partner, reading the Bible, praying, spending time with your family, watching a sermon on YouTube, or partaking in some other Philippians 4:8 endeavor.

Know the consequences. One of my often-quoted passages when teaching about sexual immorality and its consequences comes from Solomon's advice to his son in Proverbs 5:3-23 (NIV). Read along with me and notice the added emphasis on God's counsel to us:

> *For the lips of the adulterous woman drip honey,*
>   *and her speech is smoother than oil;*
> *but in the end she is bitter as gall,*
>   *sharp as a double-edged sword.*
> *Her feet go down to death;*
>   *her steps lead straight to the grave.*
> She gives no thought to the way of life;
>   her paths wander aimlessly, but she does not know it.
> Now then, my sons, listen to me;
>   do not turn aside from what I say.
> *Keep to a path far from her,*
>   *do not go near the door of her house,*
> *lest you lose your honor to others*
>   *and your dignity to one who is cruel,*
> *lest strangers feast on your wealth*
>   *and your toil enrich the house of another.*
> *At the end of your life you will groan,*
>   *when your flesh and body are spent.*

You will say, "How I hated discipline!
  How my heart spurned correction!
I would not obey my teachers
  or turn my ear to my instructors.
And I was soon in serious trouble
  in the assembly of God's people."
Drink water from your own cistern,
  running water from your own well.
Should your springs overflow in the streets,
  your streams of water in the public squares?
Let them be yours alone,
  never to be shared with strangers.
May your fountain be blessed,
  and may you rejoice in the wife of your youth.
A loving doe, a graceful deer—
  may her breasts satisfy you always,
  may you ever be intoxicated with her love.
Why, my son, be intoxicated with another man's wife?
  Why embrace the bosom of a wayward woman?
For your ways are in full view of the LORD,
  and he examines all your paths.
The evil deeds of the wicked ensnare them;
  the cords of their sins hold them fast.
For lack of discipline they will die,
  led astray by their own great folly.

Did you catch what Solomon was conveying to his son? In essence, he was suggesting the grass is not greener on the other side. Yes, the woman you are lusting over is attractive. She may say all the right things and seduce you with her persistent pleading (Proverbs 7:21, CSB), but the consequences of your actions are far-reaching. (One of the most unfortunate implications for married men is that you sever the bonds of oneness between you and your spouse.) Men, we know this is an area in which most of us struggle. Rebuke the enemy's lie that "one little look won't matter," because you and I both know the damage believing that lie can cause.

As I close this section, I strongly encourage you to have a conversation with your wife about your sex life—as uncomfortable as this may be. Discuss each other's sexual needs, level of satisfaction with your sexual encounters, and whether you are tempted to look outside the confines of your home for sexual fulfillment (that includes trying to get your sexual needs met on your phone or computer). Perhaps you could consider lovingly explaining to your wife that fulfillment of your sexual needs within your marriage will help you to guard against temptation in this area.

The devil has made this topic one that is taboo to discuss—even between two people who should know everything about one another (recall, two become one flesh)—because he knows this is a place where he can divide the marriage relationship. Get comfortable being uncomfortable and have these conversations now before you go down a path you will regret.

Conflict resolution

Speaking of uncomfortable conversations, I want to take a moment to discuss conflict in marriage. When two imperfect people are living under one roof, conflict is bound to arise. What we need to do is acknowledge this fact, then understand how we can navigate our way through disagreements for the glory of God.

Identify your enemy. You may say, "Well that's easy; my enemy in any marital conflict has to be my wife, right?" Absolutely not! The devil would love for you and your wife to see each other as the enemy because when we do so, we approach conflict trying to gain victory over the other (and truthfully, when that occurs, nobody wins). However, in Ephesians 6:12 (NIV), Paul clearly states, "our struggle is not against flesh and blood, but against the rulers, against the authorities, against the powers of this dark world and against the spiritual forces of evil in the heavenly realms." In other words, our sole enemy in a conflict is the devil himself. So, when marital conflict arises, first understand you and your bride are on the same team working against a common enemy who desires to sow seeds of discord in your marriage.

Know the appropriate time to address conflict. The moment of an initial disagreement may not be the ideal time to work toward a resolution. Psalm 4:4a (ESV) declares, "Be angry, and do not sin." Think about instances when you initially became angry toward something or someone. Chances are you felt your blood boiling inside. Now, do you think that is the appropriate time to calmly work through differences with your wife? Probably not. Instead of gratifying the desires of the flesh by lashing out at your spouse, take some time away from each other to calm down, then come back together at an agreed-upon time to work through the issue. Take time to resolve the conflict, even if it takes you all night to do so.

Know the appropriate time, yes, but do not let it linger unresolved. God's Word says you should "not let the sun go down while you are still angry, and do not give the devil a foothold" (Ephesians 4:26b-27, NIV). The enemy of our souls would love for us to ignore disagreements, thus allowing resentment to manifest. Don't allow him to have that victory.

Fight fair. First Peter 4:8 (NIV) proclaims, "Above all, love each other deeply, because love covers over a multitude of sins." When working through a challenge, avoid the temptation to bring up the past or say, "you never," "you always," or "this is just like when you…" Using those words shows you are still holding on to previous sins your spouse has committed. Paul says in 1 Corinthians 13 love "does not keep a record of wrongs" (v. 5, CSB). If we are to love our wives as Christ loved the church, we need to treat them the same way God treats us, remembering their sins no longer (Isaiah 43:25).

Acknowledge your part of the conflict. I have heard it said that when there is a horizontal conflict between you and your wife, there is almost always a vertical conflict between you and God.[74] Think about that for a moment—marital conflict abounds because one person does not agree with the other. More than likely, the root of the disagreement is due to one or both spouses' sense of pride and refusal to deny themselves to work toward a resolution. Pride and love of self are in direct contrast to a lifestyle of obedience to God (Proverbs 8:13; James 4:6), which consequently breaks our fellowship with Him. As a result, conflict will permeate our relationships if we are not willing to recognize and repent of our own sinful actions and behaviors.

Initiate resolution, even if you didn't start it. You may very well be saying, "But I didn't start it; why should I be the one who tries to resolve it?" First, I would challenge you to stop thinking like a toddler—pointing the finger at his sibling. Secondly, I would remind you of the truth in Romans 5:8 (NIV; emphasis added): "But God demonstrates his own love for us in this: *While we were still sinners, Christ died for us.*" Aren't you glad God didn't wait for us to seek reconciliation with Him? Instead, He sacrificed His own life (denied Himself) to be restored to His bride. Why aren't we willing to do the same?

Leave and cleave. Recalling Genesis 2:24 (NIV), God's Word says "a man leaves his father and mother and is united to his wife, and they become one flesh." Despite this direction from God, so many married couples still run to their parents at the first sign of trouble. I would submit this tendency is in large part due to a couple's inability to accept the truth of this verse in Genesis. When man and woman become husband and wife, it is time for them to work through challenges together—not run to their mom and dad to fight their battles. Another piece of outstanding wisdom we received in our pre-marriage counseling was that Amy and I should always put the family we were creating ahead of the family we were coming from. Your wife needs to know you choose her over your parents—especially in conflict. Do not ever let her doubt that for a moment.

I praise God that Amy and I have not had many conflicts, but when we do, we understand there is a stark contrast between handling conflict the devil's way (e.g., avoiding, yelling, fighting), as opposed to God's way. Second Corinthians 10:3 (NIV) says, "For though we live in the world, we do not wage war as the world does." Ponder how you and your wife have handled previous disagreements between one another. If change is needed, begin with these aforementioned steps, and you will be well on your way to turning conflict into productive opportunities to strengthen your marriage!

To those who are not married...

This chapter has focused on a man's role as a husband, but to those reading this who are not married, I want to offer you some encouragement as well.

Start praying now for your future wife. Pray that God will reveal Himself to her in His timing, that He will draw her close to Him, and that He will protect her, keep her pure, give her a heart for Him, and make clear to her a purpose for His Kingdom.

Prioritize inward qualities over outward ones. First Samuel 16:7b (ESV) says, "man looks on the outward appearance, but the LORD looks on the heart." Proverbs 31:30 (NIV) reinforces this key point: "Charm is deceptive, and beauty is fleeting; but a woman who fears the LORD is to be praised." When looking for a future mate, identify a woman who is a fellow believer, has a kind heart, possesses a gentle and quiet spirit, and understands God's intended role for her in your relationship. Those traits will last far beyond the outward beauty that may initially attract you to a woman.

Don't settle and miss God's best for your life. Abraham was 100 years old when Isaac—the son whom God promised to him 25 years earlier—was born (Genesis 21:5). Do not fall for the devil's lies that "you are too old to get married" or "all the good ones are gone." Continue to trust God to provide you with your mate in His perfect timing. And remember, for some men, singleness IS God's best plan for their life, as it was for Paul (1 Corinthians 7:8).

Keep your dating relationships pure. Hopefully you read through the romance section in this chapter, where I discussed in detail God's design for sex being reserved for husband and wife. My advice to you is to not put yourself in a position to fall victim to the sin of sex before marriage that so easily entangles many men. Keep the lights on, stay out of the bedroom, and avoid being alone with a woman in a compromising position if you know this area is a struggle and temptation for you.

Whether you are a single man in search of your bride-to-be, a married man of 60 years, or somewhere in between, we can all glean wisdom from God's expectations of us as men in marriage—particularly as it relates to being more intentional about loving our mates (or future ones) as Jesus loves us. Whether we realize it or not, wives are looking to husbands as the image-bearers of Christ. We should not take that lightly and thereby diminish their understanding of our Savior. Of course, we will not represent Him perfectly, but our lives should be characterized by faithfully pointing to Him. Our marriages will be blessed, our communities will be blessed, our nation will be blessed, our world will be blessed, and most importantly, our God will be glorified when men step up and assume this hefty responsibility. My prayer is that you will tap into the only Source who is able to sustain you in this quest, and I ask you to pray the same for me.

Questions to Consider

1. Is there any unresolved conflict you need to address with your spouse?

2. Are you being tempted to commit sexual immorality? If so, share those temptations with your spouse and discuss how you can partner together to overcome those struggles.

THIRTEEN

Father:
Best-laid Plans

When Amy and I got married, we thought we had it all figured out. She would work for the first few years of our marriage, then stay home with the children we were going to have around that time. To keep our timeline intact, shortly after our third anniversary we began the process of trying to have children. Months of "trying" passed, but with no success. Months turned into a year, and we grew pretty discouraged. After all, our three-year plan was not materializing the way we intended. I thought to myself, "God, did you miss the memo we faxed up to you? You're not helping us check off the boxes here."

As I type out that last paragraph and recall Proverbs 16:9 (NIV), I cannot help but laugh. In this verse, Solomon says, "In their hearts humans plan their course, but the LORD establishes their steps." God had something different—something infinitely more special—in mind for us and our family-to-be. We will get to that in a moment, but for now, I want to continue sharing with you an awesome testimony of God's mighty power.

After a year of frustration, Amy's doctor referred us to a fertility specialist. We went through some pretty invasive and embarrassing medical procedures to finally receive some shocking news from the doctor, who told us, "There is no way you two will be able to biologically conceive a child without medical intervention." When Amy asked me what I thought about the doctor's counsel, I did not have a peace about pursuing fertility treatments. (Please understand I am not making a blanket statement about whether Christians should or should not seek medical interventions for infertility—I am just telling you our story.) I felt like God was telling us to wait, so that is what we did.

Years began piling on top of one another, and we faced the same struggles so many couples understand too well. We wondered why some friends seemed to get pregnant so easily when it seemed so hard for us. We celebrated their joyous baby news while wrestling with disappointment over our unmet longings. There was a time of some bitterness, resentment, sadness, and fear—what if we could never have children? My wife had always dreamed of being a mom, and she was heartsick over her hope deferred. It was hard for me to watch, but God had given me confidence that the right thing for us to do in this situation was to wait on Him.

Slowly, gradually, something started to happen. Nothing was changing physically about our circumstances, but at the same time all of this was going on around us, God was doing a work inside us. Amy was invited to join the women's Bible study at our church that I mentioned previously. It ignited in her a newfound excitement to read, really believe, and apply the Word of God. I also joined a small group at church where God began growing me. We both started waking up early to pray and study the Scriptures. We started hearing God speak to us. We began changing things about our lives to align with His standards. And at some point, before we realized it, our desire for God eclipsed our desire for children. Don't get me wrong; we still wanted children. We prayed every day together that God would entrust us with a child. But instead of bitterness, we experienced peace. Instead of resentment, contentment. Instead of sadness, joy. Instead of fear, anticipation. The more time passed, the more convinced we grew that God's plan for us was good, that we could trust Him, and that He was fully capable of granting us children naturally if and when it was His right timing.

There are so many stories I could share from this time in our lives. David says in Psalm 40:5b (NIV), "Were I to speak and tell of your

Father: Best-laid Plans

deeds, they would be too many to declare." Trying to share our testimony feels just like this—it would be impossible to recount all the details of how God was working in and through our situation for His glory and our good.

So with the caveat that I am skipping a great deal of the story, I will pick up in August of 2017. This husband and wife—who would have been unrecognizable to themselves five years prior when they "decided to get pregnant"—were getting ready for bed. As I slid under the covers, I heard Amy in the bathroom flushing the toilet and brushing her teeth. Moments later, she came out of the bathroom, toothbrush still in her mouth, smiling a smile I had never seen before. She beamed with surprise as she held out a pregnancy test with a cross. Not a line. A cross. Of all the tests she had taken through the years, we had never had a cross before. Just a line. We were excited, but it felt surreal. Could it be true? Amy confessed, "I bought this test on the clearance aisle at Publix, so it could just be expired or something!" So instead of rejoicing and praising God as a man of faith would, I said, "Take another one!" We laugh now as we remember this story. She took two more tests. Two more crosses.

I will never forget that precious night. We knelt on our bathroom floor and praised the God who had proven Himself bigger than medicine—the Master Physician! But He had done more than give us a baby. Through these years and this trial, He had given us Himself. By the way, a year and a half later, we found out that we were pregnant with another child—God had entrusted to us another blessing for which we are so thankful!

Amy loves to share Philippians 3:8a (NIV) when we tell this story: "What is more, I consider everything a loss because of the surpassing worth of knowing Christ Jesus my Lord." Nothing compares to the surpassing excellence of knowing Christ. He is the prize. He is the greatest gift. But to our children—I want you to know that you are our gifts from the Great Giver. You are a miracle from God. I love you. I am so grateful for you. And I want you to always know—when the wisdom of this world says something is impossible—nothing is too hard for God!

Looking back, I can most definitely see God's providential and protective hand at work during our season of infertility. If we had children at the time we wanted to, there would potentially have been an immense battle in our marriage over Amy desiring to stay home but me not feeling like we could afford to make that a reality. During the "waiting" years, though, God provided opportunities in my career that did make it possible. Spiritually, God used that season to prepare us to raise children in a God-honoring and God-fearing home. Relationally, we were able to enjoy some wonderful experiences as husband and wife that we would not have otherwise been able to pursue if our "perfect" timeline had come to fruition. God's ways are higher than ours (Isaiah 55:9), and we can always see so clearly on the other side of our season in the valley. Please trust Him while you wait.

Now, I share that testimony with you for a couple of reasons: 1) I want our boys to know how God was already working in their lives long before they picked up this book, 2) I want to encourage those who may be going through similar seasons that God sees your hurt, will comfort you, is with you, and will not leave you, and 3) I want to convey to you that this is a very special section for me to write. So with the pleasantries out of the way, let us shift our focus to what God expects of us as fathers.

Questions to Consider

1. In what way have you made a plan for your life without consulting God?

2. As you look back over your walk with God, can you see times when He was protecting you from a thing you thought you wanted?

3. Spend time meditating on whether you really believe Christ Himself is the greatest gift. If not, ask God to help you deepen your desire to know Him.

FOURTEEN

A Father's Most Important Mission

Full disclosure—when Amy and I found out our first child was going to be a boy, my mind immediately conjured up dreams of afternoons at the baseball park, teaching him how to swing a bat, throw a ball, field his position, and learn to love the game as much as I do. I dreamt of long nights at the field, coaching his team to a city-league championship, taking him out for a celebratory dinner afterward, and telling him how proud I was of him—because of his athletic achievements. Then God brought about a strong conviction, as He reminded me that my most important mission as a father is not to be my son's all-star coach or even his biggest fan. Nor was I to live out my dreams vicariously through him. No, my most important purpose as a father is to share the Gospel (i.e., Jesus Christ and Him alone) with him. Then secondly, I was to help him grow in his knowledge of God and what it means to live a life dedicated to Him and His calling (i.e., discipleship).

Men, please join me in accepting this most important mission together, as we do not need to spend our energies and efforts wholly devoted to raising our children to become the next great CEO, businessperson, athlete, politician, doctor, lawyer, or _____ (you fill in the blank of a worldly expectation you may have of your children). Rather, our priority focus ought to be serving as fathers whose purpose is to raise future generations who know God personally and experience Him daily. We begin this journey by representing our children's Heavenly Father to them.

Emulate their Heavenly Father to them

When I was a little boy, I remember writing my dad notes, telling him he was "the best dad in the world." I am sure it warmed his heart to know how highly I thought of him, but with all due respect to my dad, I was wrong. It wasn't that the best dad in the world lived down the street or played baseball on the grandest stage; no, I have come to realize the best Dad in the world is my Heavenly Father.

Admittedly, I have been guilty of falling into the trap of wanting our children to adore me, but the only One our children should be adoring is God Almighty. Though we will surely fail at times, our job is to point to Him, and with the Holy Spirit's help, we can more accurately do so by fulfilling the forthcoming fatherly roles.

Teacher and equipper. In Ephesians 6:4b (ESV), Paul states we should "bring [our children] up in the discipline and instruction of the Lord." As fathers, we must teach our children the way they should go and redirect them when they stray from that path. We spent a great deal of time in the first chapter discussing God's plan of salvation, so I will not rehearse it for you again here. However, I would submit the first teachings our children need to hear and comprehend are that God loves them so much that—despite their propensity to misbehave—He wants to remain in a relationship with them. Yet in order to do so, Jesus had to die for their sins, and they must confess Him as Lord.

A common question I hear among men with young children is: "When do I know my child is ready to confess Christ as their Savior?" Although I do not have the specific answer to that question, I would encourage you to never squelch the Holy Spirit's work in your child's life by dismissing the probing questions they ask, or worse, ignoring their desire to accept Jesus into their heart because you think they are too young. There is no Bible passage setting an age limit (young or old) for salvation, and I praise God for that!

If you do not feel equipped to answer the questions your children are asking of you, enlist the help of a church staff member who is more comfortable speaking with young children about this decision. This is the most important decision your children will ever make; DO NOT PUT THIS OFF (yes, I am yelling)!!

In addition to teaching the way of salvation to our children, we also need to ensure they are equipped with the knowledge needed to live according to God's standard. To learn how to do so, let us study Moses's exhortation in Deuteronomy 6:6-9 (NIV):

> These commandments that I give you today are to be on your hearts. Impress them on your children. Talk about them when you sit at home and when you walk along the road, when you lie down and when you get up. Tie them as symbols on your hands and bind them on your foreheads. Write them on the doorframes of your houses and on your gates.

The Hebrew word for *impress* in this passage denotes the idea of teaching diligently.[75] As you read the remainder of these verses, you can see what this practically entails. This is not just a call to open up your Bible on Sunday mornings for church. This is a methodical approach to ensuring your children are equipped with God's wisdom and knowledge for any situation they may encounter.

Everywhere they turn, while in our homes, our kids ought to be trained in the Truth. For example, did your son have a bad day at school? Remind him of Jesus's words in John 16:33 (NLT): "Here on earth you will have many trials and sorrows. But take heart, because I have overcome the world." Did someone spread false and malicious gossip about your daughter on social media? Point her back to Galatians 1:10, which reminds us to consider whether we are seeking the approval of God or men. Did your son get unfairly passed up for a promotion he worked years to earn? Hebrews 4:13 reminds us that nothing is hidden from God, and one day, those who do evil will be held accountable for their actions. Did you get a call from your child that she has been diagnosed with cancer? Paul tells us in 2 Corinthians 4:16-17 (NIV) to "not lose heart. Though outwardly we are wasting away, yet inwardly we are being renewed day by day. For our light and momentary troubles are achieving for us an eternal glory that far outweighs them all."

Do you get the point? When our children come to us for guidance, we ought to respond to them just the way God does with us—with His wisdom that will equip them with the knowledge needed to navigate the perils of this world. The easiest way to do this will be for you to have a vibrant walk with God yourself. These responses will become your default counsel—the natural overflow of your relationship with God.

Along with offering biblical truths to help our children overcome inevitable trials and tribulations, we must also ensure our precious ones are equipped with a workable, applicable knowledge and overview of Scripture. To do so, incorporate Bible readings and scripture memory lessons into your daily routines with your children. Lead your family in devotions once a week. Remind them of how much God loves them and the story of Jesus's loving, sacrificial, atoning death for their sins. Your family might consider memorizing a set of catechisms; we review *The New City Catechism for Kids*[76] each day at breakfast with our children.

The point is this—be intentional about removing worldly influences and replacing them with teachable moments from God's Word. Begin when they are young, and build it into your family culture. Focusing on teaching God's Word at the expense of cultivating earthly, fleeting, temporary skills may not earn you a reputation as the coolest dad on the street. But is your aim to be "cool" by the world's standards anyway? Or, is your goal to be told "Well done, good and faithful servant" (Matthew 25:23a, CSB) by our Creator when He examines how you shepherded those entrusted to your care?

I would also add one more suggestion before we move on to the next aspect of bringing up our children in the instruction of the Lord. Read this passage from Joshua 4:

> When the whole nation had finished crossing the Jordan, the LORD said to Joshua, "Choose twelve men from among the people, one from each tribe, and tell them to take up twelve stones from the middle of the Jordan, from right where the priests are standing, and carry them over with you and put them down at the place where you stay tonight."...And Joshua set up at Gilgal the twelve stones they had taken out of the Jordan. He said to the Israelites, "In the future when your descendants ask their parents, 'What do these stones mean?' tell them, 'Israel crossed the Jordan on dry ground.' For the LORD your God dried up the Jordan before you until you had crossed over. The LORD your God did to the Jordan what he had done to the Red Sea when he dried it up before us until we had crossed over. He did this so that all the peoples of the earth might know that the hand of the LORD is powerful and so that you might always fear the LORD your God" (vv. 1-3, 20-24, NIV).

As I read God's Word to our children, I anticipate them saying, "Dad, how have you and Mom experienced God like those guys—Noah, Moses, Joshua, Jonah, and Paul?" We discussed earlier ways in which our family has experienced God, and undoubtedly you have examples you could have included there as well. Should you have a list, you have a great start in recounting God's faithfulness like the Israelites in the passage we just read. Take time to physically mark—however you want to—the times you have experienced God moving on your behalf. For Amy and me, we have a large bowl of stones with words written on them to remind us of God's faithfulness in our lives, and we look forward to the day our children begin asking what those stones mean. Just like Joshua and the Israelites, we can point back to God's goodness—bringing honor and glory to Him by passing down these experiences to our next generation—and thereby help strengthen the faith of our children in the process. To God be the glory!!

Model. As fathers, we must not merely teach God's Word to our families. Instead, our children ought to be able to follow our example of leading a disciplined, God-honoring life as well. I love the story of PGA Tour golfer Phil Mickelson, who learned to play golf from his father. (Yes, I know I just talked about how we ought not to focus on temporal skills, but the example fits.) His father was right-handed, as is Phil. Yet if you notice Phil's swing, he hits the golf ball from the left side. When asked about how Phil learned to swing left-handed, take note of his father's response (emphasis added):

> "He went right over to his spot, re-gripped the club left-handed and swung the way he visualized my swinging it in front of him. That is how he became left-handed as a golfer while being right-handed at everything else. *He was watching my swing as if he was looking into a mirror and he mimicked it.* That's the way he saw the swing. He didn't know right from left and that was just how he visualized the swing being done."[77]

Did you catch that? At an early age, Phil didn't know right from left. He simply saw what his dad was doing and mimicked it to a tee (no pun intended).

We must heed Jesus's words in Matthew 23:3 (NIV) and practice what we preach. Otherwise, we are nothing more than the hypocrites that Jesus goes on to condemn throughout that chapter. Here is a good practice to implement: as you teach God's Word to your children, pray God would reveal if you are in step with the same principles you are teaching to your children.

Your children watch and listen to you more than you know. Be sure there is consistency with what they hear about our great God and see represented through you. Otherwise, when they grow older, they will either 1) not want anything to do with that sort of lifestyle if it is anything close to what they experienced in their home or 2) have a misguided perception of what it is like to live as a Christian. I would submit none of you want either of these outcomes for your children, so let us all strive to ensure our words AND our actions are aligned with God's Word.

Discipliner. In Proverbs 3:11-12 (NIV; emphasis added), Solomon encourages his son to "not despise the LORD's discipline, and do not resent his rebuke, because *the LORD disciplines those he loves, as a father the son he delights in.*" There are a couple of implications from these two verses. First, God disciplines those He loves (look no further than the first sin of Adam and Eve in Genesis and God's subsequent banishment of the two from the Garden of Eden), and second, a father is to discipline his children.

As a young boy, I remember there were many instances when my parents disciplined me in some form or fashion. I assure you, these acts of discipline stuck with me the next time I was tempted to misbehave. Hebrews 12:11 (ESV) comes to mind when I think of these times: "For the moment all discipline seems painful rather than pleasant, but later it yields the peaceful fruit of righteousness to those who have been trained by it."

As fathers, we have a responsibility to lovingly steer our children back to God's design for their lives—holiness. However, many fathers would rather be liked by their children than endure moments of friction. Too often we view our children as friends, as opposed to little ones who God has entrusted to our care to raise up to know, obey, love, and serve Jesus. It is not uncommon in our culture to see dads abandoning this responsibility, which creates an environment where the children—not God—run the home.

We have all witnessed this scenario play out in the checkout line of a grocery store. You are behind a family whose child is pleading with their father for a candy bar (by the way, VERY strategic product placement by stores). When the little one doesn't get her way, she starts screaming. Because the child knows she runs the home, she knows that rather than stopping her unwanted behavior in its tracks, the father will buy her the candy bar to keep her from causing a scene. You may ask, "What's the big deal?" Well, over the years, a lack of discipline initially manifested in the form of a candy bar purchase may very well turn into an entitled, spoiled teenager who expects the world to give her anything she wants when she makes a fuss. You and I both know that young adult is in for a rude awakening that could have been prevented with a father's discipline early on in her life.

Now, I am not saying it is wrong to buy your kid a candy bar. However, if we are doing things to appease our children because we do not want to be inconvenienced with taking the time to discipline them, we are doing nothing more than rewarding their misbehavior. By doing so, we also are condoning that behavior in the future. Read these words from Proverbs 22:6 (CSB): "Start a youth out on his way; even when he grows old he will not depart from it." Helping your child choose the correct path starts now by ensuring that when they veer off course they are redirected back to True North (Jesus). It feels really hard to endure in a power struggle with a toddler, but—based on Godly wisdom and counsel Amy and I have received—it is not nearly as hard as fighting with a teenager who never learned to respect parental authority.

If you are still reluctant to administer discipline to your children, let me reinforce this expectation with one more verse, this time from Proverbs 13: "Whoever spares the rod hates his son, but he who loves him is diligent to discipline him" (v. 24, ESV). Dads, I am not saying you hate your children, but if you refuse to discipline them, God's Word suggests otherwise. Take action while your children are still under your roof, thus producing a solid foundation that will withstand the devil's attacks once they leave your nest. To get us started, here are seven tips for administering discipline in our homes.

1. Make sure you and your spouse are on the same page. Luke 11:17 (ESV) records Jesus saying, "Every kingdom divided against itself is laid waste, and a divided household falls." Matthew Henry states of this verse, "it is an allowed maxim, confirmed by every day's experience, that no interest can stand that is divided against itself; not the more public interest of a kingdom, nor the private interest of a house or family." [78] Remember, you and your wife are to be one flesh and a united front (Genesis 2:24)—particularly in issues such as discipline. Take time to discuss and agree with your spouse on what you will discipline, how you will discipline, and who will administer the discipline. Otherwise, you may find your kids act one way in front of one parent while acting totally different in front of the other. That yields children who are applauded for trying to cover up their sin instead of experiencing the wonderful grace and forgiveness of our Lord and Savior.

2. Don't ignore misbehavior. In 1 Samuel 2 (NIV), we read about a high priest, Eli, and his sons, Hophni and Phinehas. The Bible refers to the young boys as "scoundrels" in verse 12, and in verse 17, we get a glimpse into why they were noted as such: "they were treating the Lord's offering with contempt." Eli knew about the sins of his sons, and although he tried to caution them against their sinful acts, there is no record they paid attention to these words of warning (vv. 23-25). As a result, a prophecy came against the house of Eli where his strength—and that of his household—would be cut off, to the point where "no one in [Eli's] family line will ever reach old age" (vv. 31-32). Further, the two promiscuous sons would die on the same day as a result of their disobedience and disdain for God's commands.

As I read that passage, I have to wonder what led to the point where the two sons did not listen to their father's counsel. Was it that Eli overlooked so many of his sons' previous sins that he didn't have any credibility when he tried to speak up? Was it that this father had made idle threats before and not followed through on discipline? Had he been so consumed with his ministry to the Temple that he neglected his kids? We cannot be sure, but we can discern the sons did not have a healthy respect for their father—a respect that ought to have been cultivated from years of loving discipline. Let this serve as a cautionary tale, motivating us to put in the hard, laborious work of addressing misbehavior, no matter how small (or big) the actions may be. I encourage you to do all you can as a father to avoid raising a Hophni or Phineas, thereby allowing generations coming after us to endure the consequences of your inability to act when the need arose.

3. Be consistent with your discipline. Ephesians 6:4a (ESV) commands fathers to "not provoke your children to anger." The Amplified Bible translates the opening part of this verse: "do not exasperate them to the point of resentment with demands that are trivial or unreasonable or humiliating or abusive; nor by showing favoritism or indifference to any of them."

Think about this scenario for a moment. You were recently punished at work for coming in a few minutes late, only to learn a colleague in the same department—with the same supervisor—was not disciplined for arriving even later than you. Pretty frustrating, isn't it? Or perhaps you were scolded one day for being tardy, but two weeks later, your boss didn't say a word to you as you walked past his office 15 minutes later than your arrival time weeks before. You probably walk on eggshells because you do not know which boss you will get on any given day.

The same is true with our children. If you favor one child over another by turning a blind eye to the sins of one while dutifully enforcing God's standards with another, the latter is going to be embittered sooner rather than later. Or, if you get upset about your children talking back to you one day, then laugh it off on another occasion, how will your children know what to expect from you as it relates to what is right or wrong? Here's the point—God never wavers regarding sin. He hates sin (Proverbs 6:16-19), and sin has consequences (Romans 6:23a). If we are to represent our Heavenly Father to our children, we need to be consistent with this responsibility.

4. Do what you say you are going to do. If I had to guess, you have been around a family whose parents tell their misbehaving son, "If you do that again, I'm taking that toy away from you." 32 times later, the toy being used as a battering stick on little brother is still in the older brother's hands, and the parents are frustrated to the point of yelling. Jesus tells us in Matthew 5:37 (NKJV) to "let your 'Yes' be 'Yes' and your 'No,' 'No.'" If your child knows something is wrong, do not threaten to punish him the next time he does it; punish him then. Remember, we are supposed to be representing God to our children. His words have never failed to come to fruition, and ours should not either.

5. Be prompt on discipline. Think back to our grocery store example for a moment. Little Susie is causing quite the scene in the checkout line. You resist the urge to reward her misbehavior, telling her instead that discipline is coming when you get home. You finally make it through the checkout line, stroll out to the parking lot, load the groceries into the car, drive 15 minutes home, take several minutes to unload and put away the groceries, and then remember you had promised Susie discipline was forthcoming. Susie is off playing with her dollhouse when you come barging in and try to administer discipline, only to hear Susie say, "What did I do Daddy?" She is asking that question because our kids' attention spans are shorter than ours, and they tend to forget what they did wrong 45 minutes prior.

So, even if it means leaving your groceries in the checkout line and going straight to the car to discipline your child, do so. Yes it is inconvenient, yes it is unpleasant, yes that means you will have to make another trip to the store for groceries, but what is more important—your convenience or your child learning right from wrong? If it's the former, I challenge you to remember Luke 9:23 and be willing to deny yourself of your conveniences for the sake of those God has entrusted to you. I may note here that families with young children need to build in margin to allow for these formative moments. If your calendar is overflowing and you seem to always be on the go, it will be more challenging to discipline promptly and consistently.

6. Do not discipline when you are angry. Even though discipline needs to be prompt, we do not need to punish in the midst of anger. Just like we discussed in the section on conflict resolution with your spouse, think back to times in your life when you have been really angry. You can feel the blood rushing through your veins, adrenaline flowing, and feeling like you have supernatural strength. To be sure, this is NOT the time to discipline your children, as you may say or do something that inflicts pain well beyond what is helpful. Our intent with discipline is never to physically (or emotionally) harm. Instead, our goal is to steer our kids back onto the right path by helping them to understand their behavior is wrong. You simply want to ensure the pain of disobedience outweighs the pleasure of the sin, so your child decides the misbehavior is not worth doing again. Check your motives before you move forward with discipline to ensure you are in the right state of mind.

7. Always point them to the Truth. Speaking of motives, disciplining our children should always end with pointing them to God's standard of holiness for our lives, to our inability to ever measure up to that standard, and to the only One who can restore our broken fellowship with God. We do so by replacing lies behind their misbehaviors with God's Word—just like Jesus did with the Pharisees in Matthew 23. The passage is rather lengthy, so I won't include it here, but I highly recommend you take the time to read it. In this discourse, there are several instances when Jesus first identifies the Pharisees' sin, then shows them the way of the Truth. Take verses 25 and 26 (CEV) for instance: "You Pharisees and teachers are show-offs, and you're in for trouble! You wash the outside of your cups and dishes, while inside there is nothing but greed and selfishness. You blind Pharisee! First clean the inside of a cup, and then the outside will also be clean." Let Jesus's example here be our guide when we are disciplining, as we not only need to tell our children what they did wrong, but also should show them truth from the Bible that illuminates the correct way to think, speak, and behave.

The author of Hebrews had it right when he penned the words that no discipline is pleasant at the time (Hebrews 12:11). It is not enjoyable (at least I hope it's not in your case), and it is not easy. But the fruit of your labor is found in the latter part of this verse in Hebrews: "Later on, however, [discipline] produces a harvest of righteousness and peace for those who have been trained by it." Let's give our children the advantage in life of learning to be people who are pleasant to be around. The benefits to them will be innumerable. Simply put, if we want men and women of God to blossom out of our homes, we must be willing to discipline our children. What is standing in the way of you getting started?

Affirming love...

Now with that said, we dads tend to give attention to disciplinary issues more readily than acknowledging our children's longing for affection from us. To help us combat this tendency, here are some ways we can nurture our kids by meeting their need for fatherly love and affirmation.

With our words. Do you like to be told you do a great job at work? After diligently preparing for a project, a nice pat on the back by your supervisor probably means a great deal (although I'm sure you are thinking a nice financial bonus would be nice, too—more on that in the next chapter on work). How about at home? Is it reassuring that your wife tells you how much she loves you and is so thankful for you? Perhaps you worked for hours out in the yard and you come inside to receive a tender kiss and a "Thank you for keeping our house looking so nice." These sorts of affirmations are good for us, as Proverbs 16:24 (NLT) confirms: "Kind words are like honey—sweet to the soul and healthy for the body." So now that we have established how much we still desire the affirmation of others, how much more so do you think our kids need to hear us tell them we love them and are proud of them?

With our affection. First John 3:18 (CSB) says, "let us not love in word or speech, but in action and in truth." Our affirming words should not be lip service, but should instead be supported with actions validating our love for our children. Hug and kiss your children. Shed your macho persona, and do not let the only time you touch your children be times when you are disciplining them.

With our presence. Do you remember from our previous discussions on faith and courageous leadership that God is always with you? God takes His role of being ever-present to His children extremely seriously, so why don't we take our responsibility to reflect this trait of God's character as seriously with our children? I was startled to come across some research by Dr. Urie Bronfenbrenner, who found the average middle-class father spends *37 seconds* with his children on a daily basis.[79] Thirty-seven seconds. It may have taken you longer to read the opening paragraph of this section than most men spend with their children each day.

Most of these men may assume their wife is to be the one who should shoulder the primary responsibility of raising the children. Or worse, they have given no thought at all to who is spending the majority of time teaching and training them. If you fall into that category, I want to challenge you to consider whether those tending to your children on daily basis have a personal interest and investment in their long-term well-being. I cannot encourage you enough that we desperately need a generation of fathers to rise up and exercise leadership in this matter.

In his book *Raising Kingdom Kids,* Dr. Tony Evans speaks to this idea when he says, "There is no quality time without quantity time."[80] How can we discipline if we are never home? You will find that your children respond more favorably when you need to be stern if you have stored up memories of playful fun and an established affectionate, loving relationship. Discipline from a distant dad is rarely productive. How can we teach our children when we only have time to kiss them goodnight? How can we affirm our children if we don't ever spend quality time speaking to them? The simple answer is we can't. Yet, as fathers, we continue to excuse our absence in the home by saying, "I am working all of these hours to provide a quality life for my family," "I just need some time to myself," or "my wife is better at all that stuff than I am." Let me gently rebuke any of those thoughts with some wise words Jesus shared with Peter in Matthew 16:23a (ESV), when the latter was buying into the lies of the devil: "Get behind me, Satan!" Please listen to me—the devil would love to take the spiritual leader away from the home and confuse the roles of man and woman to your children. Do not let him have a foothold in your home!

Young children and adolescents do not connect the dots that your absence from the home every night while you work late means you love them. No, they interpret those late nights away from home and similar things as "My dad is not here when I need him, so he must not love me." And if they think that way about their earthly father, imagine the difficulty (although not impossibility) they will have accepting the fact that their Heavenly Father loves them. Your presence at home has long-lasting—even eternal—benefits, so make it a priority to be present and available to your children consistently. Read on for a handful of behaviors to consider implementing.

1. Pray for your family before you leave for work. I began incorporating this discipline into our family's daily routine last year. My wife will tell you it is one of her favorite times of the day and has made a huge impact on the way she starts the day with our kids. Yes, we may pray for our children during our personal, private time with God, but there is something about praying aloud for them when they can hear us. If you know your child is anxious about her test at school that day, what do you think makes more of an impact—telling her to go pray about it or praying on her behalf before she goes off to school? Do not let the only time your kids hear you pray be when you sit down and rush through a prayer of thanksgiving before you eat.

2. Answer the phone when they call or text. If you are like me, once you head off to work, you start thinking through all the things that have to get done that day. Email this person, call this one, tackle this project, make some progress on this issue, and so on. Before you pull into the parking lot, the to-do list is a mile long. Then the workday officially starts and more gets piled onto your plate. You feel like you are doing all you can to just tread water. Then you receive a text or a call from your child saying, "Daddy, I need to talk to you." If you ignore that text or put him off until you get home from work—whether you realize it or not—you are telling that little boy that work is more important than him. Granted, you would never say that to his face, but your actions speak louder than words when it comes to your time. The paperwork can wait; so, too, can a meeting with the boss. Work should not come before your family, so do not let your actions intentionally or unintentionally suggest otherwise.

3. Leave work at work. I am a task-oriented individual. Every time I take a personality test, this is where I score the highest. I like to get the job done, and I like to get it done now. So I understand your frustration when it is time to clock out for the day and there is still work to be done. We tend to pack up the laptop, throw it in our satchel, and take care of it when everyone goes to bed for the night. But the reality is, that project is all we can think about over family dinner and time with the kids before they go to bed, which leaves us unable to be focused, present, and available to those who love us (and need us) the most. Work will still be there in the morning. Wait until then to finish the job and be present (in body and mind) for your most important ministry in the home.

4. Tuck your kids in at night. If you implement the first suggestion of praying for your family before you leave for work, then tuck your kids in at night, your prayers will be the first and last words your children get to hear daily. Don't you love that thought? This can also be a sweet time for you to talk with your children about their day. Ask them for prayer needs they saw throughout the day, where they saw God at work, or any tangible needs they (or you all as a family) can meet. Start and finish their day with their eyes and ears fixed on Jesus.

5. Allow your kids to join you on the course or in the deer stand. If you do not play golf or hunt, that does not mean you are exempt from this recommendation. The point is this—your children look up to you, and probably long for the day when they get to join you for one of your favorite recreational hobbies. Do not buy into the devil's lie that this time is sacred for you to enjoy alone or with your friends. Some of my fondest memories as a kid were attending Houston Astros games in the Astrodome with my dad. He loved the game, and because of him taking me along so many times, I grew to love it, too. The fellowship is a tremendous benefit for a father with his child, but more importantly, the trust that is built by time spent together could reap eternal benefits years down the road as your child begins asking questions about a saving relationship with Jesus.

God first

I would be remiss if I did not add one more piece of advice to fathers before I close, as we all would be wise to heed Abraham's example in Genesis 22. If you are not familiar with the story of Abraham, God promised him and his wife a son in their later years of life—a child for whom they had so desperately yearned for years. As you can imagine, overwhelming joy filled their hearts when young Isaac was born to them. But while Isaac was still a young boy, God told Abraham to take this child of promise and sacrifice him on an altar. To Abraham's credit, he marched forward in obedience, right up to the point when he "took the knife to slay his son" (v. 10, NIV); it was then an angel of the LORD stopped him before he carried out the sacrificial act.

While our children are precious to us, we can learn from Abraham that our relationship with and obedience to our Heavenly Father still comes first in our lives. Do not let anything, or anyone, come in the way of obeying God. If that means coming home early from a baseball tournament so you can lead your family into church on Sunday mornings, be willing to prioritize God over your children. If that means not letting your teenager spend time with a boy who may have ulterior motives, be willing to be disliked by your daughter for the sake of obeying God. God first, wife second, children next. Keep that priority list in order.

As I think about our responsibilities as a Godly father, I fully acknowledge I have only scratched the surface. Even still, what I have provided to you is a hefty duty. Psalm 127:3 (CEV) reminds us, "Children are a blessing and a gift from the LORD." If we truly believe that, we will assume the tremendous task of shepherding our children in a way that encourages them to know, love, and serve God. We do so by teaching, equipping, and disciplining them as our Heavenly Father does to and for us, affirming them, and being fully present and available to them. There will be times we fail, and when you do, ask your children for forgiveness. In fact, what better opportunity to explain the hope and message of the Gospel to them!

Questions to Consider

1. By your words and actions, what are you teaching your children?

2. In what way do you need to make more time for your children?

3. Are your disciplinary actions done more because you are inconvenienced by your child's misbehavior, or due to your desire for them to know, love, and serve God?

FIFTEEN

Worker:
Not About Me

I had been serving in my role at the community college where I work for several years when my boss announced his retirement. Upon his announcement, many of my peers looked to me to fulfill his responsibilities. In fact, when the job vacancy was posted—with a salary substantially higher than what I was bringing home—the summary of duties looked exactly like what I was doing for the College at the time. I had several colleagues ask me if I was leaving the school because the job summaries looked so similar. So taking both of these factors into consideration—the increase in salary and comparable job descriptions—I determined in my mind that this was the next step in God's promotion of me in my career. But a "funny" thing happened during that process.

Shortly after submitting my application for the vacated position, I received a phone call to set up an interview with the search committee. I felt like the initial interview was a roaring success, as many of the questions related to the work I was already doing. Yet another affirmation God was orchestrating all the details to make this promotion a reality (at least that is what I thought). Then came the waiting…and the waiting…and even more waiting. Through some back-channel communications, I was able to determine final interviews and a hiring had already taken place—without me. What's more, the person selected for the job was someone from outside the College who—on his first few days on the job—told me I would need to help him learn many of his responsibilities because he did not have prior experience with many of the areas that he was now overseeing.

To be totally transparent with you, I was furious. I was bitter. I was hostile. I was jealous. Honestly, I was in a dark place. Through no fault of his own—because he was a good man—I took out my frustration on my new boss by criticizing him to others (instead of befriending and helping him), venting frustration to anyone who would listen, and seeking job opportunities at other institutions that would result in similar pay increases. I did all of this without talking to God. I went down a path of self-destruction with inward motives of self-promotion. Interestingly, the timing of this trial at work coincided with the first year of our infertility struggle—before our hearts had been stirred and changed by God. But looking back, we see how the unraveling of our plans brought us to our knees.

One day during this period of self-pity, I was called into the President's office. "Good," I thought, "maybe she realizes the College made a mistake and is about to offer me that promotion *I deserve*." Instead of patting me on the back, apologizing for the grief I felt I had endured, and telling me about plans to promote me, she had a different message: "Shape up or be shipped out." She had heard about my grumbling, was fed up with it, and told me if word got back to her that my behavior continued down this path, she would see to it that I would have no choice but to seek employment elsewhere. Oh, how Jesus's words in Luke 14 make so much sense in retrospect:

> When he noticed how the guests picked the places of honor at the table, he told them this parable: "When someone invites you to a wedding feast, do not take the place of honor, for a person more distinguished than you may have been invited. If so, the host who invited both of you will come and say to you, 'Give this person your seat.' Then, humiliated, you will have to take the least important place. But when you are invited, take the lowest place, so that when your host comes, he will say to you, 'Friend, move up to a better place.' Then you will be honored in the presence of all the other guests. For *all those who exalt themselves will*

be humbled, and those who humble themselves will be exalted" (vv. 7-11, NIV; emphasis added).

As I left the President's office that day, I was scared. I was embarrassed. Most importantly, I was humbled. It was then that God showed me I was focused on self-glorification while hiding behind righteous motives like trying to make enough money for Amy to stay home. But in reality, it was all about me and how quickly I could climb the ladder of success.

Do not buy into the devil's definition of success

If we look around, it does not take long to see how society defines success, and unfortunately, I bought into this lie of the devil. The enemy deems one "successful" by what car you drive, by how many bedrooms and square feet you have in your house, by how many club memberships you possess, and by how many zeroes are at the end of your paycheck. Patrick Morley refers to this "pursuit of a beautiful, wrinkle-free life" as the "rat race," whereby we let something other than God's Word dictate the standards by which we ought to live. According to Morley, these standards of success come from a concept referred to as *psychological obsolescence.* In it, society is "programmed to consume, because the dominant economic theory employed in America is a progressively greater consumption of goods is beneficial." He goes on to suggest that the more possessions we consume—thus increasing our material standard of living—the lower our moral, spiritual, and relational standard of living becomes.[81]

If you think about it, this makes sense, as the more we are chasing after material possessions, the more we need to focus on earning money to do so. As a result, we expend a considerable amount of energy on our careers to make more money and be deemed a professional "success." Then when we get home, we are worn out and have little time or emotion left in the tank for our wives or children. Relationships suffer, our time with God suffers, church attendance suffers, and spiritual growth for our families and ourselves suffer—all for the sake of pride or an extra dollar.

Here is what the devil does not tell you about his standard of success. In Ecclesiastes 5:10 (NIV), Solomon states, "Whoever loves money never has enough; whoever loves wealth is never satisfied with their income. This too is meaningless." Here is a man who had more wisdom and riches than any other king in the world (1 Kings 10:23), yet he was still not satisfied with the number of possessions at his fingertips.

Many think they would finally be content with just a little more. Let me illustrate this fallacy for you: for the past few months, money has been tight, and you have barely had enough to pay your bills. Your car is due to be replaced, but you cannot find the money to take on another car payment. You think to yourself as you lay your head down for the night, "If I could find a job paying just $5,000 more a year, I could buy a new car and everything would be great!" Well, as luck would have it, a job offer for just that amount comes your way the next morning, and you jump at the opportunity. Upon receipt of your first paycheck at this higher salary, you rush out and "purchase" (i.e., agree to make 60 payments on) a new car, expending all of your additional income.

All is great for four months, but then your water heater bursts at your aging home, leaving you with thousands of dollars in damage. You think again, "If I could find a job paying just $3,000 more, we could move out of this place and into a nicer, newer house that won't have nearly as many maintenance issues to repair." Do you see what happened? Initially, you found contentment in a job paying $5,000 more, but then your standard of living quickly adjusted to your new level of income as you rushed out to purchase a new car. But then the next material possession you overly value started accumulating dust and rust, and you quickly grew discontent with your new income level. So now, you move the bar a little higher. And unfortunately, when we are chasing after the world's standard of success, the bar never completely settles, as there will always be the next car, house, job, hobby, television, tool, grill, or home improvement project on which to spend money. As my father-in-law often says, "the cost of living is whatever you make, plus 10 percent."

Now, I am not saying we cannot be ambitious in our professions, even desiring a higher salary in the process. But as you consider your ambitions, I would also encourage you to consider your motives. If you have a temporal frame of reference—thinking about promotion of self to enjoy the riches of this world—discontentment will come soon after you settle into your advanced role. However, if you maintain an eternal perspective with eyes laser-focused on glorifying God, your ambitious heart is in the right place. (By the way, you can quickly gauge your intentions by considering whether you intend to use your expanded influence to represent Jesus to more people and steward the additional resources to advance His Kingdom purposes. Anything else and your motives may be misplaced.)

We have to make a conscious decision to not follow the cultural standards of success, even if it does not make sense or goes against what feels good to us. If you still are not convinced, perhaps this excerpt from 1 John 2 will bring it home for you: "Do not love the world or anything in the world. If anyone loves the world, love for the Father is not in them. For everything in the world—the lust of the flesh, the lust of the eyes, and the pride of life—comes not from the Father but from the world. The world and its desires pass away, but whoever does the will of God lives forever" (vv. 15-17, NIV). Put your hope in temporary successes, and your desires will quickly pass away. However, if you refocus your energy on glorifying God in your profession, the rewards you receive from Him will endure forever! Learn from my mistakes as we read on together about God's design for our work.

Questions to Consider

1. How do you define success?

2. Do you struggle with negativity, bitterness, or a critical spirit at work? What's behind those struggles?

SIXTEEN

A New Mission for Work

In Genesis 2:15 (NIV), "The LORD God took the man and put him in the Garden of Eden to work it and take care of it," and Genesis 1:31 tells us that all God made was good. Why do I include these two references? I want you to see that God created work, and if all God created is good, that must mean work is good. If that is the case, why do 53 percent of Americans claim to be unhappy with their work?[82] Why is the median length of time the average employee spends in their job less than five years (and for younger generations, less than four years)?[83] I am convinced too many men—even Christians—have a false perception of work, thinking their joy, purpose, and significance are tied to their title, rank, or salary. Thus, at the first sign of adversity, men flee to the next opportunity, thinking a new job will provide the satisfaction their old position could not offer (only to find more disappointment once the shine wears off their new desk).

The Bible tells us God has a different purpose for our work. We find it in Colossians 3:22-24 (NIV):

> Slaves, obey your earthly masters in everything; and do it, not only when their eye is on you and to curry their favor, but with sincerity of heart and reverence for the Lord. Whatever you do, work at it with all your heart, as working for the Lord, not for human masters, since you know that you will receive an inheritance from the Lord as a reward. It is the Lord Christ you are serving.

Let's break down this passage as we discover how God commands us to work.

Obedience. "Slaves, obey your earthly masters in *everything*" (Colossians 3:22a, NIV; emphasis added). Have you ever disagreed with your supervisor over how to handle a situation? To ask that question is to answer it, because I would suggest all of us who have had a boss have disagreed with him or her at one time or another. Disagreements are not necessarily the issue, but rather what we do afterward that may pose a problem and most certainly reflects our heart toward work. We may not always agree with our bosses, and at times, we may be right. However, we must still submit to and obey those God has put in supervisory roles over us (unless, of course, they ask us to violate God's Word). Here is some wisdom from the book of Proverbs to reinforce Paul's exhortation to obey:

> "Hatred stirs up conflict, but love covers over all wrongs" (10:12, NIV).

> "A hot-tempered person stirs up conflict, but the one who is patient calms a quarrel" (15:18, NIV).

> "A perverse person stirs up conflict, and a gossip separates close friends" (16:28, NIV).

> "The greedy stir up conflict, but those who trust in the LORD will prosper" (28:25, NIV).

When disagreements arise in our workplace, the one whose heart is set on himself (i.e., hot-tempered, hateful, greedy, stubborn) is the one who goes behind their boss's back, slandering him to anyone who will listen, and stirring up conflict (much like I did in the situation I described in the last chapter, quite frankly). But the one whose heart is set on God, even though he may disagree with his boss, will let the conflict subside in obedience and submission to his "master."

Perspective. For those who have their heart focused on God's purposes for them at work, willful obedience to their supervisor is easy. Well, it should be, because in the end, it is not a "frustrating boss who never listens to me" who I am serving, but as Paul explains in Colossians 3:24b (NIV), "It is the Lord Christ you are serving." So long as we keep that perspective—an eternal one—serving our earthly "masters" should not be a challenge, but instead a joy. When you find yourself tempted to shift your perspective to a temporal one, I would offer the following suggestions:

1. Take your thoughts captive. In 2 Corinthians 10:5 (NIV; emphasis added), Paul says, "We demolish arguments and every pretension that sets itself up against the knowledge of God, and *we take captive every thought to make it obedient to Christ.*" Tempted by the devil's lies? Pray something like this: "God, the devil is trying to tempt me with lies like 'I do not matter' and 'my voice is not heard,' but I know you see and hear me. I am choosing to take those lies from the enemy captive, turn it over to you, and trust in Your promises."

2. Pray for your boss. Do you know what I have found in my experience? The more I pray for someone, the more God endears me to that person. As I cultivate this habit, I begin trying to find specific requests I can lift up to God on that person's behalf. Then I get excited when I find something for which I can petition God on their behalf. If I have this mentality—as opposed to one that is bitter toward my boss—my time will more productively be spent focusing on how God can work in that person's life. Now say you think your boss is beyond repair (in your limited mind you think this because the truth is nothing is impossible for God). Begin praying God would tender that person's heart, open her ears to hear from you, or be willing to accept and implement ideas that are not his own. We fail to do this because either 1) we want to handle things in our own fleshly way (which never ends well) or 2) we do not believe God can change a person's disposition. Neither one is too flattering for you as a representative of God in the workplace.

3. Brag about your boss. What better way to change your perspective from inwardly focused on self to an upward focus on God than to look out for the interest of others, right? Listen, you may not always agree with your boss or jump at the chance to obey him when you disagree, but there are good qualities in your supervisor about which you can boast to others. We ought to heed James's warning when he says, "Out of the same mouth come praise and cursing. My brothers and sisters, this should not be" (James 3:10, NIV). Furthermore, Paul exhorts us in 1 Thessalonians 5:11a (NIV) to "encourage one another and build each other up." I urge you to use these principles from God's Word to change the tone of your words about your boss from condemnation to blessing.

Sincerity. If we are honest with ourselves, most of us would probably admit to working harder when our boss is around. Granted, work still goes on, but we may be more prone to talk to a colleague, check in on social media for a moment, or update our checking account when management is not present. According to Colossians 3:22, though, our work ethic in front of our supervisors should not change when they depart the room. C.S. Lewis once said "integrity is doing the right thing, even when no one is watching."[84] I would submit there is Someone who is always watching us and knows our true motives. Read the following:

> "For the eyes of the LORD range throughout the earth to strengthen those whose hearts are fully committed to him" (2 Chronicles 16:9, NIV).

> "For your ways are in full view of the LORD, and he examines all your paths" (Proverbs 5:21, NIV).

"O LORD, you have searched me and known me! You know when I sit down and when I rise up; you discern my thoughts from afar" (Psalm 139:1-2, ESV).

"The LORD knows man's thoughts" (Psalm 94:11a, HCSB).

With these passages in mind, always be mindful—even though your boss may not be in the room to see if you are giving your best effort—God Almighty is in the office, room, or assembly line with you. He is watching to see if you will honor Him with your work, or instead, opt to slack off to appease your fleshly desires (know I am convicted even as I write this). Be sincere men of integrity by working with all of your heart, no matter the audience.

Reverence. Common synonyms of the word *reverence* include worship, admiration, and respect.[85] In the context of Colossians 3:22-24, out of "reverence for the Lord," we ought to express our gratitude and appreciation to our Jehovah Jireh (that is, "the LORD will Provide"—Genesis 22:14, NIV). Admittedly, you may be in a dead-end job with no prospects of promotion, you may find yourself in a position grossly underpaying you for the work you perform, or you could even find yourself in a hostile environment with a verbally abusive supervisor. Yet in each of those situations, 1) you have a job (more than many can say) and 2) you have a sphere of influence to whom you can represent Jesus Christ consistently. If for no other reason, be grateful to your Provider for giving these opportunities to you.

Particularly if your peers at work share your frustrations, your gratitude to God will shine through, and they will notice something different about you. Get yelled at by the boss in front of others for no reason today? Thank God for the chance to show His grace to someone else. Accidentally delete a project you have been working on for months? Thank your Heavenly Father for the opportunity to fine-tune it a second time. Someone snag your parking spot today? Thank God for a chance to spend more time in His creation walking to the office today. Do you get it? First Thessalonians 5:16-18 (NIV; emphasis added) commands us to "Rejoice always, pray continually, *give thanks in all circumstances*; for this is God's will for you in Christ Jesus." By thanking God in reverence for everything that comes your way, your perspective remains focused on Him and how you can bring Him honor and glory, regardless of how mundane or frustrating your workday may be.

Diligence. Shortly after I came into my current position, I began using the motto "1-0," which represents my desire to win every moment. More specifically, in every interaction I have with students, faculty, staff, colleagues, and community partners, I approach those moments with a winning mentality. On the surface, this sounds like just another leadership term I could use as the basis for a TED talk, so allow me to dive a bit deeper into this motto for a bit.

With a transformed perspective on my work—no longer seeking to pad my résumé to glorify myself—my new mission is to glorify God in all I do. Jesus exhorts us in Matthew 5:16 (NLT) to "let your good deeds shine out for all to see, so that everyone will praise your heavenly Father." My motivation to win every moment is not so I can get a pat on the back. Instead, my attitude toward work is grounded in the belief that others will see what I am doing, begin to ask questions as to WHY I am working in that manner, then come to realize the true motivation and inspiration for my diligent approach to my job (to glorify God).

Rewards. According to a recent survey, 46 percent of employees believe they are not paid enough for the work they perform.[86] You may very well be in that group. If you are, please let me redirect your focus to Jesus's words in Matthew 6:19-21 (NIV), when He says, "Do not store up for yourselves treasures on earth, where moths and vermin destroy, and where thieves break in and steal. But store up for yourselves treasures in heaven, where moths and vermin do not destroy, and where thieves do not break in and steal. For where your treasure is, there your heart will be also."

Remember, those who work according to God's standards will receive an eternal inheritance and reward from the Lord (Colossians 3:24). However, if your mind is focused on your wages—which are here today and gone tomorrow (2 Corinthians 4:18, TM)—you will be disappointed in what you bring home in the form of a paycheck. Sure, you may be content for now, but just wait until that next big project is stacked on your plate without additional compensation. The discontentment will inevitably come when your eyes are fixed on the temporary. Alternatively, when we are following the counsel of Paul in Colossians 3:2 (NIV), we "Set [our] minds on things above, not on earthly things." It is then our focus moves away from earthly wages and is redirected to the inheritance we will receive from the Lord as a reward for our dutiful, God-honoring service.

In sum, it does not matter whether you are the president of a Fortune 500 company, middle management, a front-line worker, or somewhere in between. I need you to know the way we approach our work is to be the same for all of us. God has a purpose for us in our specific role so we, as Christian men, may serve as Christ's ambassadors to those we interact with during our daily work routine. You are to work in an obedient, reverent, diligent, sincere, and eternally-focused manner so your colleagues may see Christ exemplified through you and say, "I want whatever he has." That is where God is glorified and you begin to store up for yourselves treasures in Heaven where nothing can destroy (Matthew 6:20).

What if I'm the boss?

We have spent a great deal of time in this chapter speaking about your role as a worker, an employee, or a subordinate, but I want to take a few moments before we close to speak to those who have supervisory responsibilities. Granted, many of the truths we have reviewed are applicable in all situations. However, if you find yourself in a leadership role at work, I would like to offer you some practical suggestions for how to strengthen your representation of Christ.

Care for your sheep. In John 10:14 (NIV), Jesus refers to Himself as "the good shepherd." Therefore, if we are to effectively serve as Christ's ambassadors to those we lead, we should have a good understanding and application of what it means to be a shepherd. Jesus gives us an idea of what this role looks like in Luke 15:4-6 (ESV): "What man of you, having a hundred sheep, if he has lost one of them, does not leave the ninety-nine in the open country, and go after the one that is lost, until he finds it? And when he has found it, he lays it on his shoulders, rejoicing. And when he comes home, he calls together his friends and his neighbors, saying to them, 'Rejoice with me, for I have found my sheep that was lost.'" In John 10:28b (NIV), Jesus says of His sheep, "no one will snatch them out of my hand." So whether it is ensuring all of your sheep are accounted for (e.g., showing concern for their sick child), guiding them back to where they ought to be (e.g., offering constructive criticism to improve work performance), or protecting their safety and well-being (e.g., ensuring your team is not subjected to unfair work conditions), a good shepherd cares for his sheep.

Be willing to be inconvenienced. Continuing with this shepherd analogy, Jesus states in John 10:15 that—as the good shepherd—He lays down His life for His sheep. As leaders, every day ought to be marked by a denial of self for the sake of others. Jesus commands His disciples in John 15:12 (NIV) to "Love each other as I have loved you." In the next verse, He makes a statement that the greatest love we can display comes by laying down our lives for those we love. So we see here Jesus commanding His followers to love each other; then He goes on to convey how that love manifests—through sacrifice. The application for a boss is to be the one who serves the final customer when everyone else is exhausted after a long day of work. Or, be the first to volunteer to pick up a task for an employee who will be out sick for a few days. And just like Jesus lays down His life "of my own accord" (John 10:18, NIV), we need to take the initiative (don't be forced) to serve.

Be accessible, approachable, and responsive. One final shepherd illustration, then we will move beyond the pasture. Jesus says in John 10:27 (NIV), "My sheep listen to my voice; I know them, and they follow me." The implication here for supervisors is we must be communicative with those we serve. In other words, how will our employees recognize our voice if we lock ourselves in our office and never speak to them? Ensure your employees know they can openly share with you and are confident you will not ignore their concerns. In my leadership role, I enjoy conducting weekly check-in calls with each member of our team. Doing so helps deepen my knowledge of those I serve—to include being sensitive to their struggles, fears, anxieties, and goals—which in turn, equips me to adjust my leadership style to meet their needs.

Do not ask anyone to do something you are not willing to do. Heading into the final discourse of His Sermon on the Mount, Jesus told His audience, "in everything, do to others what you would have them do to you" (Matthew 7:12, NIV). That reminds me of a story my mom once told me about her time as a store manager for a large retail company. She came in the day after Christmas to prepare the store for its early opening, only to find the bathrooms had not been cleaned. In my immaturity, I asked her to whom she delegated this task, and her response has always stuck with me. She said, "I picked up the mop and cleaned the bathrooms myself because I always want my team to know I am willing to get in the trenches with them." What a wonderful example of managing in a way that reflects the heart of Jesus to your sphere of influence.

Empower others. Have you ever been in a job where you have been micromanaged? If you have, then you know it is not a pleasant feeling to have someone constantly looking over your shoulder and giving you instructions on your every move. Please know there is a better way to lead, and we can gain knowledge on how to do so from Jesus's empowerment of His disciples. In Matthew 10:1 (NIV; emphasis added), "Jesus called his twelve disciples to him and *gave them authority* to drive out impure spirits and to heal every disease and sickness." Then in Matthew 10:5-6, we read about Jesus sending them out with specific instructions to fulfill His intended plans.

Applying Jesus's leadership philosophy to our management opportunities, then, we would be wise to 1) identify the appropriate employee for the task at hand, 2) provide them with our expectations for the project, 3) give them the resources needed to fulfill the mission, then 4) send them off and get out of their way to let them do the work we entrusted them to do. You know there is not much more deflating than to have a boss micromanaging your every move. You would not want that to be your work environment, so do not make it someone else's.

Do not repeat what has frustrated you in the past. I credit my wife for this management principle because every time I would come home and complain about something a former supervisor said or did, she would encourage me with, "Someday you'll be in that position, and when you are, remember this so you won't make others feel that same way." Proverbs 26:11 (NIV) states, "As a dog returns to its vomit, so fools repeat their folly." Now, we may not be repeating our own folly when we commit the same acts that frustrated us at one time or another. However, if you commit the same mistakes you observed with clarity in someone else, you are not much different from the fool who is likened to a dog trying to digest its own regurgitation.

If you are like most Americans, you spend at least 40 hours of your week (almost ¼ of your time and nearly half your waking hours) at work. I think you would agree this is a substantial amount of time to spend dreading what you do, who you are around, and how much you earn. Instead, when we approach our work from a perspective that God has us exactly where we are and doing precisely what He wants us to do during this season (Ephesians 2:10), our outlook becomes much brighter. Join me in committing every moment to God and seeking to glorify Him in all we do, so others will see our good works and glorify our Father in Heaven. It is no longer about me, but He! That is what our work should be all about.

Questions to Consider

1. Do some introspection this week and consider why you do what you do. If your answer does not start with "to glorify God," you need to reassess your priorities.

2. How would others describe your work ethic? Do you do just enough to get by, or do you give a full day's work every day?

3. If you are a supervisor, do you aim to serve others, or have them serve you?

SEVENTEEN

Friend:
Two are Better than One

Research shows some startling trends comparing the way men and women approach friendships. Dr. Ronald Riggio provides us with a summary of these differences when he states that, "On the whole, women tend to invest more in maintaining their friendships—calling friends regularly, meeting more frequently, etc. Men, on the other hand, don't feel as much need to stay in touch."[87] I know I do not put enough emphasis on this role, and most of the men I speak with would admit they don't do so either. Many—myself included—suggest they are too busy with family and work to cultivate meaningful, biblical friendships.

Yet God never intended for us to isolate ourselves. Proverbs 18:1 (ESV) says, "Whoever isolates himself seeks his own desire; he breaks out against all sound judgment." Note also Paul's introduction to the Roman soldier's shield in Ephesians 6:16 (ESV), when he states, "In all circumstances take up the shield of faith, with which you can extinguish all the flaming darts of the evil one." Ancient Rome was known for its military prowess, in large part due to the weaponry Roman soldiers carried with them into battle. One specific piece of battle armor, a soldier's *scutum* (i.e., shield), was particularly helpful in keeping the brigade safe and secure. "The [curved] shape of the *scutum* allowed packed formations of legionaries to overlap their shields to provide an effective barrier against missiles…(such as arrows or objects thrown by defenders on walls)."[88] Be sure to catch this—alone the *scutum* provided adequate protection for the Roman soldier, but when locked together with a fellow brother's shield in battle, his defense was almost impenetrable.

Guys, it is not God's design for us to go into battle alone. First and foremost, we have His Holy Spirit working in us to steer us back on the right path. But He has also gifted us with brothers in Christ with whom we can lock arms and wage war together against the devil and his schemes. So with that in mind, let us discover what embodies true biblical friendship, according to God's Word.

What a friend is

As I write this chapter, my heart is heavy because of the recent passing of our family dog. He had been with Amy and me since we were dating, a span of almost 15 years. They say a dog is man's best friend, and I do find it interesting I am writing this section on the heels of his passing. However, with all due respect to our beloved canines, God does not intend for four-footed pets to be our go-to source for camaraderie. Rather, God's design is for you and me to enter into meaningful, loving, Christ-like relationships with our fellow man (John 13:34-35), and we can glean much of what He expects from these relationships from a passage in Mark 2. Read the following:

> A few days later, when Jesus again entered Capernaum, the people heard that he had come home. They gathered in such large numbers that there was no room left, not even outside the door, and he preached the word to them. Some men came, bringing to him a paralyzed man, carried by four of them. Since they could not get him to Jesus because of the crowd, they made an opening in the roof above Jesus by digging through it and then lowered the mat the man was lying on. When Jesus saw their faith, he said to the paralyzed man, "Son, your sins are forgiven." Now some teachers of the law were sitting there, thinking to themselves, "Why does this fellow talk like that? He's blaspheming! Who can forgive sins but God alone?" Immediately Jesus knew in his spirit that this was what they were thinking in their hearts, and he said to them, "Why are you thinking these things? Which is easier: to say to this paralyzed man, 'Your sins are forgiven,' or to say, 'Get up, take your mat and walk'? But I want

you to know that the Son of Man has authority on earth to forgive sins." So he said to the man, "I tell you, get up, take your mat and go home." He got up, took his mat and walked out in full view of them all. This amazed everyone and they praised God, saying, "We have never seen anything like this!" (vv. 1-12, NIV).

Knowing each other's needs. Biblical friendships go beyond surface-level conversations to reveal the state of each man's well-being. Take the passage we just read, for instance. Although the paralyzed man had a physical need very much visible to all, his four friends must have known the man *desired* to be healed. Now how would they have known this desire if they hadn't engaged with him in meaningful, heartfelt conversations?

As men, we are great at sharing. Really, we are. Get us talking about last night's football game or our last hunting or golfing trip, and we could carry on a conversation for quite some time. But if we ask one another to go deeper and open ourselves up to more vulnerable dialog, we clam up pretty quickly. Please know I am not averse to light-hearted conversations, as there is a time and place for that. However, we need to acknowledge that biblical friendship goes beyond superficial discussions to ask questions like "What is God doing in your life?"; "Where are you struggling in your daily walk?"; "How can I specifically pray for you right now?"; and "Where do you feel like the devil is attacking you?"

In Galatians 6:2a (NIV), Paul says to "carry each other's burdens," but how will others know our burdens if we are not willing to share? Listen, I get it. It is not easy opening up and telling someone else where you are weak. We, as men, have bought into the devil's lies that we are the only ones going through a certain temptation, and if we reveal our weaknesses to someone else, he will think less of us, judge us, and broadcast our secrets to the entire world on social media. Do not buy into the fallacy that you are the only one going through something. Chances are, the men with whom you share your vulnerabilities have gone through or are currently going through the same temptations and can empathize with you. So rather than responding to the question, "How are things going?" with a "Good" and moving on, be transparent with like-minded men God has placed in your life to encourage you to stand firm in the faith (1 Corinthians 16:13).

Helping to meet each other's needs. Looking back on the four friends bringing their paralyzed comrade to Jesus for healing, we see very clearly that biblical friendship does not just take time to learn about each other's needs, but actually does something about them. I am reminded of the lyrics from Tracy Lawrence's song *"Find Out Who Your Friends Are."* You may recall some of the lyrics, but one of the verses that jumps out to me is below:

> Somebody's gonna [sic] drop everything
> Run out and crank up their car
> Hit the gas, get there fast
> Never stop to think 'what's in it for me?' or 'it's way too far.'
> They just show on up with their big old heart
> You find out who your friends are.[89]

Just like the four men we read about in Mark 2, true friends do not count the cost of helping each other. Forget about the labor, time, or money involved; biblical friends see a need and do whatever it takes (including making a hole in the roof of a house and creating a contraption to lower their friend to the physician) to get one another the help needed. First John 3:16-18 (ESV) reminds us of a truth we have discussed many times already but bears repeating in this context: "By this we know love, that he laid down his life for us, and we ought to lay down our lives for the brothers. But if anyone has the world's goods and sees his brother in need, yet closes his heart against him, how does God's love abide in him? Little children, let us not love in word or talk but in deed and in truth." Quite simply, if you have an ability to meet a friend's need—or know someone who can—yet turn a blind eye to your brother's calamity, the Bible poignantly questions whether God's love resides in you at all. Pretty convicting stuff for this guy who needs to do a better job in the friend department.

Bringing each other back to the Truth. Biblical friendships certainly are a blessing from God. When we are willing to open ourselves up and go deeper, we find comfort and encouragement to know we are not alone in our struggles and temptations. We expose our needs to others and thank God they are willing to do whatever it takes to meet those needs. But to take it a step further, we need to be more like the four men in Mark 2, bringing our wounded friend to (or back to) Jesus for healing and restoration. In Christian circles, this process is often referred to as accountability. "Wait a minute," you ask, "how is being accountable to someone else a good thing?" Well, if we are approaching our lives from a temporary, worldly perspective, accountability is not something you welcome. The world (i.e., the devil) says we should be accountable to no one, and unfortunately, this myth is becoming more and more the majority opinion. However, men with an eternal perspective—seeking to honor and glorify God in all they do—welcome accountability. Here is an example of accountability from God's Word, this time from 2 Samuel 12:1-13a (NIV):

> The LORD sent Nathan to David. When he came to him, he said, "There were two men in a certain town, one rich and the other poor. The rich man had a very large number of sheep and cattle, but the poor man had nothing except one little ewe lamb he had bought. He raised it, and it grew up with him and his children. It shared his food, drank from his cup and even slept in his arms. It was like a daughter to him.
> "Now a traveler came to the rich man, but the rich man refrained from taking one of his own sheep or cattle to prepare a meal for the traveler who had come to him. Instead, he took the ewe lamb that belonged to the poor man and prepared it for the one who had come to him."

David burned with anger against the man and said to Nathan, "As surely as the LORD lives, the man who did this must die! He must pay for that lamb four times over, because he did such a thing and had no pity."

Then Nathan said to David, "You are the man! This is what the LORD, the God of Israel, says: 'I anointed you king over Israel, and I delivered you from the hand of Saul. I gave your master's house to you, and your master's wives into your arms. I gave you all Israel and Judah. And if all this had been too little, I would have given you even more. Why did you despise the word of the LORD by doing what is evil in his eyes? You struck down Uriah the Hittite with the sword and took his wife to be your own. You killed him with the sword of the Ammonites. Now, therefore, the sword will never depart from your house, because you despised me and took the wife of Uriah the Hittite to be your own.'

"This is what the LORD says: 'Out of your own household I am going to bring calamity on you. Before your very eyes I will take your wives and give them to one who is close to you, and he will sleep with your wives in broad daylight. You did it in secret, but I will do this thing in broad daylight before all Israel.'"

Then David said to Nathan, "I have sinned against the LORD."

Like David, sometimes I am blind to my sinful ways and need an outsider's perspective to point out my flaws. Biblical friends are not afraid to confront one another and point them back to God's standard of holiness, so their fellow man can recognize he has sinned against God. Solomon states in Proverbs 27:5-6 (NIV), "Better is open rebuke than hidden love. Wounds from a friend can be trusted, but an enemy multiplies kisses." Earlier in Proverbs, he proclaims, "Where there is no guidance, a people falls, but in an abundance of counselors there is safety" (11:14, ESV). Start applying God's wisdom and listen to the men He has put in your life to restore you to His Truth (and be willing to do the same for your fellow brother in Christ).

United in faith and purpose. In our referenced passage in Mark 2, did you notice Jesus referred to the men's faith as the reason the paralyzed man received spiritual healing? Think about this for a moment—at any time, one of the four men could have thrown up his hands, said the house was too crowded, and given up hope of their friend being healed. Yet each one was not only committed to the paralyzed man, but also to the Healer. They were like-minded in their faith and purpose, and their healed friend was the benefactor.

To experience true biblical friendship, men must be united in purpose. As we have discussed, that purpose is glorifying God to our spheres of influence. Sure, there may have been common interests or hobbies that brought us together, but the bond uniting us should be our passion for encouraging each other to grow in our relationships with God, thereby increasing our ability to effectively represent and glorify God in all we do.

Proverbs 27:17 (ESV) is an often-quoted verse in the context of men's ministry: "Iron sharpens iron, and one man sharpens another." The illustration here is two pieces of metal rubbing against each other, creating friction and heat (I am sure you have heard the cliché "being on fire for God"). Something else about this verse jumped out to me, though, as I was studying recently and that was the idea that both metals are the same. It is not iron sharpening aluminum; it is iron sharpening iron. Applying this verse to our lives then, we can surmise men are best "sharpened" when they are united in purpose with a like-minded Christian man. So I would ask you to consider—are your friendships marked by a desire to help your friend grow closer to God and fulfill his God-given purposes, or are you more concerned about talking with your buddies about your most recent golf outing or hunting expedition?

Friendship pitfalls

Now that we have identified God's design for friendships, let us address some pitfalls to avoid as we seek to establish meaningful, God-honoring bonds with others.

Unequally yoked with unbelievers. If we are going to experience true, biblical fellowship with each other, we must spend time with men who will sharpen—not diminish—our acumen for God's standard of living. In other words, we would be unwise to lock arms with men committed to chasing frivolous fantasies. Consider the following wisdom from the Bible:

> "Whoever walks with the wise becomes wise, but the companion of fools will suffer harm" (Proverbs 13:20, ESV).

> "Do not be deceived: 'Bad company ruins good morals.'" (1 Corinthians 15:33, ESV).

> "Do not be unequally yoked with unbelievers. For what partnership has righteousness with lawlessness? Or what fellowship has light with darkness?" (2 Corinthians 6:14, ESV).

> "Do not make friends with a hot-tempered person, do not associate with one easily angered, or you may learn their ways and get yourself ensnared" (Proverbs 22:24-25, NIV).

I often hear men trying to rationalize their time spent with those not of a similar worldview with the argument, "Well how can I reach the lost if I don't spend time with them?" While there is merit to that question, I would strongly advise you to consider your motives. For instance, you do not have to pull up a seat at the bar and have a drink with someone to share the saving message of Jesus Christ. Even if he is an alcoholic who spends most of the time at his favorite establishment, he will leave at some point to take a shower, go to work, or grab some more cash. Wait for him in the parking lot if you must, but do not put yourself in a situation where your representation of our Savior is adversely affected because you think the only way to effectively witness is to literally meet him where he is. That is a lie from the devil that puts you in a position to fall prey to temptation.

Emotional connection with women. Quick Hebrew lesson for you: in Genesis 4:1 (NASB), we read about Adam having "relations with his wife, Eve, and she conceived and gave birth." The Hebrew word for *relations* (i.e., sex) here is *yāda'*, which means to know, learn to know, reveal oneself, or become acquainted with. The word is used almost 1,000 times in the Old Testament—many times in the context of God's desire for His people to know Him.[90] I include this reference here because "True sexual intimacy, which includes the romantic ties of knowing and being known, shares much more than moments of passion. It is experienced because two people share secrets, their biology, pheromones, fears, failures, hopes, dreams, trust and even more."[91]

As married men, you can certainly see how befriending women is a slippery slope. You may think to yourself that you are just being an empathetic ear to a colleague or neighbor, but Dr. Tony Evans states, "when either married individual shares that aspect of intimacy with someone outside of the marriage covenant, he or she has broken the sacredness of the secret treasure once shared with his...spouse."[92] Oneness (i.e., two becoming one flesh) is no longer oneness when another person is brought into the equation.

Judging others. As we have established, it takes a lot for men to open up to others (even their wives). So when they finally muster up the courage to engage in conversations about their struggles, fears, and temptations, they need to know they are doing so in an environment free from judgment. Jesus reminds us in Matthew 7:1 (ESV) to "Judge not, that you be not judged." A couple of verses later, He admonishes those who judge by referring to them as hypocrites who ignore their own sin while condemning others for their iniquities (Matthew 7:3-5). Guard against the tendency to convict someone of their "junk," knowing you have your own mess that you are dealing with inside you. If you are still high on your perch—looking down on the sins of others—let me remind you of the following verses:

> "The LORD looks down from heaven on all mankind to see if there are any who understand, any who seek God. *All have turned away, all have become corrupt; there is no one who does good, not even one*" (Psalm 14:2-3, NIV; emphasis added).

> "[F]or all have sinned and fall short of the glory of God" (Romans 3:23, ESV).

Yes, there are appropriate times for rebuking and holding others accountable, but as with many things we have discussed, question whether your heart is genuinely in the right place. Do you truly care about the other person's spiritual health, or are you more concerned about beating them up while they are down in an effort to lift yourself up?

Slanderous talk. Earlier, I mentioned the passing of our family dog and how many refer to canines as "man's best friend." As I think about that label for our pets, I am convinced part of the reason we cherish our dogs so much is that they—unlike humans—are a vault. Unless you own the Bush's Baked Beans dog, you can tell a dog anything and not worry about him divulging your secrets to anyone else. However, with men, we cannot say the same.

In the same manner we need to be careful not to judge others when they share with us, we also need to keep their words in confidence and avoid talking about them behind their back. We may preface the gossip with a "Bless their heart" or "I'm just sharing a prayer request with you," but that is nothing more than jargon I would expect to hear from a Pharisee, not a man walking closely with God. Proverbs 16:28 (NIV) states, "A perverse person stirs up conflict, and a gossip separates close friends." In the next chapter, Solomon reiterates his earlier wisdom by saying, "Whoever would foster love covers over an offense, but whoever repeats the matter separates close friends" (Proverbs 17:9, NIV). Then, in Proverbs 20:6 (AMP), he asserts, "Many a man proclaims his own loyalty *and* goodness, But who can find a faithful *and* trustworthy man?" Read what Bible scholar Matthew Henry has to say about this verse:

> It is easy to find those that will pretend to be kind and liberal. Many a man will call himself a man of mercy, will boast what good he has done and what good he designs to do, or, at least, what an affection he has to well-doing. Most men will talk a great deal of their charity, generosity, hospitality, and piety, will sound a trumpet to themselves, as the Pharisees, and what little goodness they have will proclaim it and make a mighty matter of it.
> But it is hard to find those that really are kind and liberal, that have done and will do more than either they speak of or care to hear spoken of, that will be true friends in a strait; such a one as one may trust to is like a black swan.[93]

When you are tempted to tell someone's secrets to another person, tell it to God. He already knows, but His Holy Spirit would love to remind you the same love He displayed on the Cross for you is the same love He has for that other person. Moreover, He would also encourage you—instead of being tempted to air their dirty laundry elsewhere—to commit to finding ways to restore that person to the standards found in God's Word. Let that—not malicious babble—be your focus.

Stealing time away from higher priorities. Biblical friendships are an important role men should prioritize. Otherwise, I would not have spent a whole chapter dedicated to the topic. However, we need to be aware of our tendency to wander from home—leaving our wife and children behind—for the sake of male-to-male fellowship. God. Wife. Children. Friends. In terms of relationships, that is the order in which we need to prioritize our time. Do not be tempted to rearrange those priorities so you can selfishly pursue a night out with the guys. Your wife and family need to spend quality time with their spiritual leader.

If you do find yourself conflicted between time with family and time with your friends, I would encourage you to maximize the time already spent away from home. Here are a few examples you could implement:

- Schedule lunch outings with your friends once every couple of weeks. Keep the reoccurring item on your calendar so you don't double-book yourself.
- Arrange a specific time each week—even on your way to or from work—when you can catch up with an accountability partner over the phone.
- Meet for an early breakfast or Bible study, long before the kids get up in the morning. Yes, I realize it may make for an early morning, but deny yourself (Luke 9:23) the extra sleep and be disciplined about meeting with other men at times when your other foundational roles are not compromised.
- Plan a family get-together to include spouses and kids on the weekend.

In other words, creatively make this role a priority, but not THE preeminent priority in your life. That time should be reserved for God and those in your home.

Two are better than one

Thus far in this section on foundational functions of manhood, we have outlined many expectations falling upon our shoulders. To be sure, it is a heavy responsibility, but isn't it also reassuring to know you are not alone as you are tempted to allow stresses, anxieties, fears, and doubts to overtake you? Are you comforted to know God intends for you to have friends who are committed to keeping you on the narrow path to following and loving God with all your heart?

If you still need convincing of why you ought to place importance on this foundational function, take heed of the following passages from God's Word:

> "Two are better than one, because they have a good return for their labor: If either of them falls down, one can help the other up. But pity anyone who falls and has no one to help them up" (Ecclesiastes 4:9-10, NIV).

> "A friend loves at all times, and a brother is born for a time of adversity" (Proverbs 17:17, NIV).

> "I long to see you so that I may impart to you some spiritual gift to make you strong—that is, that you and I may be mutually encouraged by each other's faith" (Romans 1:11-12, NIV).

It was Helen Keller who once said, "Alone we can do so little; together we can do so much."[94] When cultivated appropriately, our fellow man offers love, encouragement, and accountability to us in some of our most vulnerable and desperate times. Take note of Solomon's words in Ecclesiastes 4:10b (NIV) that were referenced a moment ago: "pity anyone who falls and has no one to help them up." I implore you—in the strongest sense—not to be alone when you fall and to make this a priority as you broaden your representation of Jesus Christ to others within your sphere of influence.

Questions to Consider

1. Are your friendships based more on common hobbies or a common Savior?

2. Are you currently in the habit of meeting with an accountability partner? If not, what is stopping you from being accountable to someone else?

EIGHTEEN

Steward:
It's all God's

Biblical stewardship is one aspect of foundational manhood that affects all other roles we fulfill. A good friend of mine, Marcus Hall, has written a wonderful book entitled *Spiritual Wealth*, which takes you on a 40-day journey of reorienting your life to serving as a steward of all God has entrusted to you: your time, talents, and treasures.[95] I highly recommend it for deeper reading on this subject, as I want to just introduce you to what it takes to be a wise steward here.

First, it would behoove us to understand the idea of stewardship—particularly from God's perspective. I hope the following example from Matthew 25:14-30 (ESV) will convince you that God entrusts resources to us intending that we invest those blessings for His purposes:

> "For it will be like a man going on a journey, who called his servants and entrusted to them his property. To one he gave five talents, to another two, to another one, to each according to his ability. Then he went away. He who had received the five talents went at once and traded with them, and he made five talents more. So also he who had the two talents made two talents more. But he who had received the one talent went and dug in the ground and hid his master's money. Now after a long time the master of those servants came and settled accounts with them. And he who had received the five talents came forward, bringing five talents more, saying, 'Master, you delivered to me five talents; here, I have made five talents more.' His master said to him, 'Well done, good and faithful servant. You have been faithful over a little; I will set you over much. Enter into the joy of your master.' And he also who had the two talents

came forward, saying, 'Master, you delivered to me two talents; here, I have made two talents more.' His master said to him, 'Well done, good and faithful servant. You have been faithful over a little; I will set you over much. Enter into the joy of your master.' He also who had received the one talent came forward, saying, 'Master, I knew you to be a hard man, reaping where you did not sow, and gathering where you scattered no seed, so I was afraid, and I went and hid your talent in the ground. Here, you have what is yours.' But his master answered him, 'You wicked and slothful servant! You knew that I reap where I have not sown and gather where I scattered no seed? Then you ought to have invested my money with the bankers, and at my coming I should have received what was my own with interest. So take the talent from him and give it to him who has the ten talents. For to everyone who has will more be given, and he will have an abundance. But from the one who has not, even what he has will be taken away. And cast the worthless servant into the outer darkness. In that place there will be weeping and gnashing of teeth.'"

Admittedly, early on in our marriage, I was much like the third servant above, in that I did not have a proper view of biblical stewardship. I thought the time, talents, and money we had available were ours to spend, hoard, and use as we saw fit. If you think similarly, click the unsubscribe button from the devil's newsletter and remind yourself of the truth from God's Word, this time from Psalm 24:1a (NIV): "The earth is the LORD's, and everything in it." Pretty clear, is it not? Everything you have is God's—not yours. And all He has entrusted to us is to be used for His glory (1 Corinthians 10:31). I am thankful God has opened my eyes over the years to realize He has not called us to clench these resources with a tight fist. Instead, he has tasked us with holding them "gently in the open palm of [our] hand—not too tightly, offering to take care of it while aware that God [has] entrusted it to [us] for a reason."[96]

Because we have already discussed a good bit about how to make the best use of our time, I will focus now on how men of God ought to best steward their finances and talents (i.e., spiritual gifts) for God's glory and to advance His Kingdom work on earth.

Stewarding our treasures

Pastor Ron Dunn once said, "In the battle of faith, money is usually the last stronghold to fall."[97] Billy Graham pronounced, "If a person gets his attitude toward money straight, it will help straighten out almost every other area in his life."[98] We often avoid this subject because we have bought into the devil's lie that the balances in our checkbooks are ours to use as we please, so let's read this passage from Luke 12:16-21 (NIV) to better understand God's point of view on "our" money:

> And [Jesus] told them this parable: "The ground of a certain rich man yielded an abundant harvest. He thought to himself, 'What shall I do? I have no place to store my crops.'
> "Then he said, 'This is what I'll do. I will tear down my barns and build bigger ones, and there I will store my surplus grain. And I'll say to myself, "You have plenty of grain laid up for many years. Take life easy; eat, drink and be merry."'
> "But God said to him, 'You fool! This very night your life will be demanded from you. Then who will get what you have prepared for yourself?'
> "This is how it will be with whoever stores up things for themselves but is not rich toward God."

From these verses, we see God does not intend for us to use the money He has blessed us with to enjoy a lavish lifestyle of self-gratification and self-glorification. Nor does He command us to hoard the entirety of our income to use later. Even still, I can hear the devil whispering in my ear now: "You have worked hard. You deserve to use that hard-earned money to buy the car of your dreams." Or perhaps he may tempt me with: "You know, you can afford that larger house; just skimp a little on what you are giving to the church each month. It's not like anyone sees your giving amounts anyway." Or even: "Man, you are good at what you do. Why aren't you out trying to earn more money to build a more luxurious life for your family?" These misconceptions from the devil are nothing more than him trying to reorient my eyes to an inward, self-centered approach of worshipping myself by trying to convince me that the money in my bank account is to be spent on gratifying my own fleshly, sinful desires.

So how do we move away from this mindset of "it's all mine" to "it's all God's"? We can start with the following action items.

Tithing. God commands us in Malachi 3:10a (NIV) to "Bring the whole tithe into the storehouse, that there may be food in my house." Since this is a command from God Almighty, this is not optional in our home—and it should not be in yours either. A tithe is 10 percent of your first fruits (Proverbs 3:9), not whatever is left over once you ensure your debts are paid and earthly pleasures are satisfied. In our family, tithing is one way to show we trust God with our finances as we give back just a portion of what He has entrusted to us.

Take note, also, of what God promises us in the latter part of Malachi 3:10, when He says, "Test me in this...and see if I will not throw open the floodgates of heaven and pour out so much blessing that there will not be room enough to store it" (Malachi 3:10b, NIV). This is the only place in the Bible where God says we can test Him on something, and I—along with countless others I know—can testify God has made good on this promise. Now please hear me—we do not tithe just so we can receive blessings from God; we do so because He has lavished His love on us, and we love Him back—so much that we are compelled to do what He commands.

Avoiding debt. When our minds are fixed on temporary matters, temporary things matter to us. For example, we see a neighbor driving a new car, and our heart longs for one as well. Or, we see our friends moving into a nice, new, larger house, and we think how nice it would be to do the same. I am reminded of an old Lendingtree commercial about a guy named Stanley Johnson, who seemed to have it all (the good life, if you will). Yet at the end of the clip, he confesses, "How do I do it? I'm in debt up to my eyeballs."[99]

In our quest to keep up with others—rather than focus our eyes on how God desires for us to steward our finances—we often amass large amounts of debt, which subsequently keeps us confined, restricted, and without any margin to meet needs God may place on our heart.

These verses from Proverbs are great reminders to delay gratification, not spend more than you have, and resist the urge to go further into debt:

> "Better to be a nobody and yet have a servant than pretend to be somebody and have no food" (12:9, NIV).

> "One person pretends to be rich, yet has nothing; another pretends to be poor, yet has great wealth" (13:7, NIV).

> "The rich rule over the poor, and the borrower is slave to the lender" (22:7, NIV).

Does that last verse hit home with you? Right after payday, do bills upon bills upon bills seem to swallow your entire paycheck? Wouldn't it be nice to reduce—or better yet, eliminate—the number of bills you owe, thus freeing up what God has entrusted to you for blessing others?

Blessing others. Now, you may be thinking, "I can afford to give God 10 percent, and because I am now out of debt, I now have 90 percent to spend as I please." However, I would remind you to consider Paul's words in Galatians 5:13b (NIV) when he says to "not use your freedom to indulge the flesh." Instead, turn your newfound financial freedom into creative ways to bless others in Jesus's name, and remember, the entirety of your account balance is God's—not just a percentage.

Jesus says in John 13:34-35 (NIV), "A new command I give you: Love one another. As I have loved you, so you must love one another. By this everyone will know that you are my disciples, if you love one another." How cool is it that God has gifted us with resources so we can turn around and lovingly share with others—all for His glory? He does not need our money to accomplish His purposes, but I think it's neat that He allows us to be part of His blessing others when we are faithful stewards of His finances.

There are over 2,000 verses in the Bible about money; for context, only about 500 verses deal with prayer and faith.[100] Jesus knew how important this matter was, which is why He advises us in Matthew 6:24 (NIV), "No one can serve two masters. Either you will hate the one and love the other, or you will be devoted to the one and despise the other. You cannot serve both God and money." Simply put, it all comes down to our perspective on ownership. If we listen to the devil, we will gratify our selfish desires as we spend "our" money to increase our standard of living. However, if we believe God is the owner of all we possess, we will embark on a wonderful journey to discover how He wants us to glorify Him by properly stewarding His treasures.

Stewarding our talents

Once you accept Jesus Christ as your Lord and Savior, God bestows specific spiritual gifts upon you with clear expectations that you utilize those talents for His glory (1 Corinthians 12:4-6; 1 Corinthians 10:31). As a dutiful steward, then, it is imperative we know the spiritual gifts that He has equipped us with and recognize how to properly deploy them, doing our part in advancing His will and glorifying Him to our spheres of influence.

Knowing your gifts. In three New Testament passages, we see a comprehensive list of spiritual gifts articulated. Read the following and see if you can identify them:

"Now to each one the manifestation of the Spirit is given for the common good. To one there is given through the Spirit a message of wisdom, to another a message of knowledge by means of the same Spirit, to another faith by the same Spirit, to another gifts of healing by that one Spirit, to another miraculous powers, to another prophecy, to another distinguishing between spirits, to another speaking in different kinds of tongues, and to still another the interpretation of tongues. All these are the work of one and the same Spirit, and he distributes them to each one, just as he determines...And God has placed in the church first of all apostles, second prophets, third teachers, then miracles, then gifts of healing, of helping, of guidance, and of different kinds of tongues. Are all apostles? Are all prophets? Are all teachers? Do all work miracles? Do all have gifts of healing? Do all speak in tongues? Do all interpret?" (1 Corinthians 12:7-11, 28-30, NIV).

"For just as each of us has one body with many members, and these members do not all have the same function, so in Christ we, though many, form one body, and each member belongs to all the others. We have different gifts, according to the grace given to each of us. If your gift is prophesying, then prophesy in accordance with your faith; if it is serving, then serve; if it is teaching, then teach; if it is to encourage, then give encouragement; if it is giving, then give generously; if it is to lead, do it diligently; if it is to show mercy, do it cheerfully" (Romans 12:4-8, NIV).

"So Christ himself gave the apostles, the prophets, the evangelists, the pastors and teachers, to equip his people for works of service, so that the body of Christ may be built up" (Ephesians 4:11-12, NIV).

There are a number of spiritual gifts God may choose to bestow upon us, and since my intention is to simply introduce you to these principles in this chapter, I will take just a moment to list them here. For a full description of each of these gifts, I recommend you visit https://spiritualgiftstest.com. You can also find a spiritual gifts inventory test on this website, which will help you identify the specific gifts God has entrusted to you.

- Administration
- Apostleship
- Discernment
- Evangelism
- Exhortation
- Faith
- Giving
- Healing
- Interpretation
- Knowledge
- Leadership
- Mercy
- Miracles
- Pastor/Shepherd
- Prophecy
- Service
- Teaching
- Tongues
- Wisdom

Before we move on, I would be remiss if I did not remind you that you will be held accountable for all God has entrusted to you—including your spiritual gifts (Romans 14:12). If you are unsure how to get started using your talents, start by asking God where He wants you to get involved. James 4:2c (NIV) says, "You do not have because you do not ask God." Seek His counsel and respond in obedience to His direction. You could also make plans to talk with a church leader about how to put your gifts to work. There are many ministries available—several of which may be aligned with the good works God prepared in advance for you to do—so be sure you are not ignoring these abilities and begin utilizing them now.

Employing your gifts properly. There are two pieces of counsel I would offer you when considering the proper use of the spiritual gifts God has entrusted to you: 1) do not use your gifts for selfish gain and 2) do not view your gifts as inconsequential.

To the former, Paul says in Philippians 2:3a (NIV), "Do nothing out of selfish ambition or vain conceit." We need to understand that these God-given talents are just that—God-given. You did not earn them, nor was it in your ability that you acquired them. "Therefore, as the Scriptures say, 'If you want to boast, boast only about the LORD'" (1 Corinthians 1:31, NLT). Recall, our life purpose should be to glorify God—not self—in all we do. Resist the devil's temptations to use God's wonderful gifts for personal promotion.

To the latter, I want to take a moment to provide you with some insight into the human anatomy. In 2011, I was having immense stomach discomfort, and after a series of tests, the doctors determined that my gallbladder was not functioning properly. In case you were curious, the average gallbladder weighs only two ounces, which equates to roughly .07% of my weight.[101] Despite its negligible size in comparison to the rest of my body, this small organ brought all of me to my knees in writhing pain. I share this to remind you that—no matter how minor you think your particular gift is in God's grander plan—the proper use of your talent is essential to a well-functioning body of Christ. This would explain why Paul states the following:

> Now if the foot should say, "Because I am not a hand, I do not belong to the body," it would not for that reason stop being part of the body. And if the ear should say, "Because I am not an eye, I do not belong to the body," it would not for that reason stop being part of the body. If the whole body were an eye, where would the sense of hearing be? If the whole body were an ear, where would the sense of smell be? But in fact God has placed the parts in the body, every one of them, just as he wanted them to be. If they were all one part, where would the body be? As it is, there are many parts, but one body.
> The eye cannot say to the hand, "I don't need you!" And the head cannot say to the feet, "I don't need you!" On the contrary, those parts of the body that seem to be weaker are indispensable, and the parts that we think are less honorable we treat with special honor. And the parts that are unpresentable are treated with special modesty, while our presentable

parts need no special treatment. But God has put the body together, giving greater honor to the parts that lacked it, so that there should be no division in the body, but that its parts should have equal concern for each other. If one part suffers, every part suffers with it; if one part is honored, every part rejoices with it (1 Corinthians 12:15-26, NIV).

Avery Willis suggests "God's purpose in giving different gifts to believers is to bind all Christians into one interdependent body."[102] God has uniquely designed each of us to play a part in His larger plan, but when we are not utilizing our gifts appropriately, the whole body—your home, your church, and the whole Christian community—suffers. As an essential contributor to God's perfect and sovereign will, do your part to know and properly use your spiritual gifts, then open your eyes to see the body of Christ strengthened and God Almighty glorified!

Only Jesus

As we wrap up this section on foundational functions, I can think of no better summary than the chorus from Casting Crowns in their song *"Only Jesus"*:

> I don't want to leave a legacy
> I don't care if they remember me
> Only Jesus
> And I, I've only got one life to live
> I'll let every second point to Him
> Only Jesus.[103]

The flesh in me wants my wife to praise me for being the best husband in the world, and my selfish inclinations long for our boys to proclaim me as the best dad. My pride would love to receive awards for being an outstanding employee, and it would be great if my ego could be inflated by my friends referring to me as the one they can count on in any circumstance or from others coming to me for guidance on how to be a better steward. When I am living a life from a worldly perspective, I put a lot of weight into these accolades from others. Yet when I am eternally focused, my foremost concern is representing my Lord and Savior—Jesus Christ—to all those within my sphere of influence. Pointing to Him in all I do—and taking advantage of the time, talents, and treasures He has entrusted to me to help others see, know, and fall more deeply in love with the Way, the Truth, and the Life (John 14:6)—is my most important function. Prayerfully, that is what I shall continue to do.

Questions to Consider

1. What would your checkbook register reveal about your stewardship of God's finances? Are you spending more to build God's Kingdom or your own?

2. Have you identified your spiritual gifts, and if so, how are you using them for God's glory?

CONCLUSION

Burn the Ships

As I think through all God has impressed upon me to share in this book, it comes back to one verse: "Whoever wants to be my disciple must deny themselves and take up their cross daily and follow me" (Luke 9:23, NIV). As Christian men, we must realize the life we live is no longer our own to do as our selfish flesh desires. Instead, our lives are to be fully committed to representing Jesus and glorifying God in all we do with all He has entrusted to us (1 Corinthians 6:20, ESV). It is a simple concept, but one of the hardest to practice. Read what Paul has to say about this in Romans 7:15-20 (NIV):

> I do not understand what I do. For what I want to do I do not do, but what I hate I do. And if I do what I do not want to do, I agree that the law is good. As it is, it is no longer I myself who do it, but it is sin living in me. For I know that good itself does not dwell in me, that is, in my sinful nature. For I have the desire to do what is good, but I cannot carry it out. For I do not do the good I want to do, but the evil I do not want to do—this I keep on doing. Now if I do what I do not want to do, it is no longer I who do it, but it is sin living in me that does it.

I am reminded of a *Seinfeld* episode where one of the characters—George Costanza—intentionally made decisions counter to his instinct. To his surprise, every decision he made thereafter was a good one.[104] In this way, we would be wise to emulate George, because our fleshly, selfish desires and instincts are rooted in sin. But when we choose to deny those dispositions, we begin seeing fruit of the life God has in mind for us.

You may think the responsibilities and expectations of a foundational man are too much to handle. You may also find yourself overwhelmed by the thought of living a life representative of Christ to those around you. If the devil is running roughshod in your mind with those filthy lies, I would invite you to take to heart Jesus's exhortation in Matthew 6:33 (NIV): "But seek first his kingdom and his righteousness, and all these things will be given to you as well."

My encouragement to you is to try the disciplines about which you have read for one year. I promise you that if you do these daily, you will not want to go back from where you came (and neither will those in your sphere of influence). Lean on the promise from God that if you draw near to Him, He will draw near to you (James 4:8). He took the first step in showing His love to us (Romans 5:8); now we must respond in faith and obedience to Him.

As you progress in this journey, know storms will come. The devil will try to discourage you and persuade you with his lies, as he knows a man whose heart is devoted to God is dangerous ammunition against the schemes he is trying to employ. To face those storms, ensure your foundation is built on the Rock—not on sinking sand. Those whose foundations are built upon the sand will crash at the first sign of trouble, but those whose foundations are built upon the immovable bedrock of Jesus Christ will never fall (Matthew 7:24-27). Granted, it is easier to build a foundation on the sand, but if your foundation is built on anything other than Jesus, it will lead to failure and destruction.

"If you are a history buff, you may know the story of [Hernán] Cortés and the burning of his ships. In the year 1519...Cortés arrived in the New World with six hundred men and, upon arrival, made history by destroying his ships. This sent a clear message to his men: There is no turning back."[105] It does not matter where you have come from. From this point forward, say goodbye to your old life, burn those old ships, and do not look back.

Notes

Introduction—Where Were You When the World Stopped Turning?

[1] Farrar. S. (2008). *God built*. David C. Cook. p. 48.

[2] Willis. A. (1997). *MasterLife: A biblical process for growing disciples.* Lifeway Christian Resources.

Chapter 2—Sanctification: My Sins Erased

[3] Hunt, T.W., & King, C. V. (2008). *The mind of Christ*. Lifeway Christian Resources.

Chapter 3—Victorious Living: Putting on the Armor

[4] Lawless, C. (2007). *Putting on the spiritual armor: Equipped and deployed for spiritual warfare*. LifeWay Christian Resources. p. 102.

[5] Blue Letter Bible. (n.d.). Nāḥam. In *Blue Letter Bible*. Retrieved February 24, 2021, from https://www.blueletterbible.org/lang/lexicon/lexicon.cfm?Strongs=H5162&t=HNV

[6] Blue Letter Bible. (n.d.). Metanoeō. In *Blue Letter Bible*. Retrieved February 15, 2021, from https://www.blueletterbible.org/lang/lexicon/lexicon.cfm?Strongs=G3340&t=ESV

[7] Lawless, C. (2007). *Putting on the spiritual armor: Equipped and deployed for spiritual warfare*. LifeWay Christian Resources.

Chapter 4—Denying Self: Saying "Yes" to God

[8] Merriam-Webster. (n.d.). Disciple. In *Merriam-Webster.com dictionary*. Retrieved February 15, 2021, from https://www.merriam-webster.com/dictionary/disciple

Chapter 5—Daily Disciplines: What Do You Put in Your Mind?

[9] Pew Research Center. (2018, June 13). *The age gap in religion around the world*. Retrieved February 19, 2021, from https://www.pewforum.org/2018/06/13/the-age-gap-in-religion-around-the-world

Chapter 6—Bible Intake: Your Daily Bread

[10] Hunt, J. (2017, February 17). *Battle ready* [Conference session]. Johnny Hunt Men's Conference, FBC Chipley, Chipley, FL, United States.

[11] Locke, C. (2020, December 27). *Fearless living*. [Video]. YouTube. https://www.youtube.com/watch?v=7UzOrLavi2w&feature=youtu.be

Chapter 7—Prayer: Your Steering Wheel or Your Spare Tire?

[12] Goodreads. (n.d.). *Ryan Blair quotes*. Retrieved February 16, 2021, from https://www.goodreads.com/author/quotes/3363420.Ryan_Blair

[13] Westfall, S. (2011, December 11). *What if you woke up today with only the things you thanked God for yesterday?* Retrieved February 16, 2021, from https://stacywestfall.com/what-if-you-woke-up-today-with-only-the-things-you-thanked-god-for-yesterday

[14] Scriven, J. M. (1855). *What a friend we have in Jesus* [Song].

[15] *My eye is not on the fog*. (2016, June 10). Christ In Our Home Ministries. Retrieved February 15, 2021, from https://www.georgemuller.org/devotional/my-eye-is-not-on-the-fog2874126

[16] Volunteer, R. A. (2016, December 5). *Answers to prayer: George Müller part 1*. Servant of Messiah Ministries. Retrieved February 15, 2021, from https://servantofmessiah.org/answers-to-prayer-part1

[17] Elevation Worship. (2017). *Do it again* [Song]. On *There is a cloud* [Album]. Provident Label Group.

[18] Queen. (1989). *I want it all* [Song]. On *The miracle* [Album]. Capitol Records.

[19] *31 prayer quotes: Be inspired and encouraged*. (2016, October 20). Crosswalk Editorial Staff. Retrieved February 15, 2021, from https://www.crosswalk.com/faith/spiritual-life/inspiring-quotes/31-prayer-quotes-be-inspired-and-encouraged.html

Notes

Chapter 8—Worship: To Whom or What is Your Praise Directed?

[20] Merriam-Webster. (n.d.). Worship. In *Merriam-Webster.com dictionary*. Retrieved February 15, 2021, from https://www.merriam-webster.com/dictionary/worship

[21] Packer. J. I. (2010). *A quest for Godliness: The puritan vision of the Christian life.* Crossway. p. 249.

[22] Morley, P. (2007). *A man's guide to the spiritual disciplines: 12 habits to strengthen your walk with Christ.* Moody Publishers. p. 65.

[23] Morley, P. (2007). *A man's guide to the spiritual disciplines: 12 habits to strengthen your walk with Christ.* Moody Publishers. p. 69.

[24] Kroft, S. (2005, November 4). Tom Brady: Part 3. *60 Minutes.* https://www.cbsnews.com/news/transcript-tom-brady-part-3

[25] Pascal, B. (1966). *Pensees.* Penguin Books. p. 75.

[26] Tomlin, C., & Whitehead, D. (2017). *Holy roar: 7 words that will change the way you worship.* Bowyer & Bow.

[27] Blue Letter Bible. (n.d.). yāḏâ. In *Blue Letter Bible*. Retrieved March 9, 2021, from https://www.blueletterbible.org/lang/lexicon/lexicon.cfm?Strongs=H3034&t=NIV

[28] Blue Letter Bible. (n.d.). hālal. In *Blue Letter Bible*. Retrieved March 9, 2021, from https://www.blueletterbible.org/lang/lexicon/lexicon.cfm?Strongs=H1984&t=NIV

[29] Blue Letter Bible. (n.d.). zāmar. In *Blue Letter Bible*. Retrieved March 9, 2021, from https://www.blueletterbible.org/lang/lexicon/lexicon.cfm?Strongs=H2167&t=NIV

[30] Blue Letter Bible. (n.d.). tôḏâ. In *Blue Letter Bible*. Retrieved March 9, 2021, from https://www.blueletterbible.org/lang/lexicon/lexicon.cfm?Strongs=H8426&t=NIV

[31] Blue Letter Bible. (n.d.). bārak̲. In *Blue Letter Bible*. Retrieved March 9, 2021, from https://www.blueletterbible.org/lang/lexicon/lexicon.cfm?Strongs=H1288&t=NIV

[32] Blue Letter Bible. (n.d.). tᵉhillâ. In *Blue Letter Bible*. Retrieved March 9, 2021, from https://www.blueletterbible.org/lang/lexicon/lexicon.cfm?Strongs=H8416&t=NIV

[33] Blue Letter Bible. (n.d.). šāḇaḥ. In *Blue Letter Bible*. Retrieved March 9, 2021, from https://www.blueletterbible.org/lang/lexicon/lexicon.cfm?Strongs=H7623&t=NIV

[34] Merriam-Webster. (n.d.). Lazy. In *Merriam-Webster.com dictionary*. Retrieved February 15, 2021, from https://www.merriam-webster.com/dictionary/lazy

[35] *9 benefits of 30 mins of exercise per day*. (2016, April 11). General Fitness. Retrieved February 15, 2021, from https://www.genesisfitness.com.au/blog/9-benefits-30-mins-exercise-day

[36] Blue Letter Bible. (n.d.). Zālal. In *Blue Letter Bible*. Retrieved February 22, 2021, from https://www.blueletterbible.org/lang/lexicon/lexicon.cfm?Strongs=H2151&t=ESV

[37] Blue Letter Bible. (n.d.). Qādaš. In *Blue Letter Bible*. Retrieved February 22, 2021, from https://www.blueletterbible.org/lang/lexicon/lexicon.cfm?Strongs=H6942&t=ESV

[38] Hunt, J. (2017, February 17). *Battle ready* [Conference session]. Johnny Hunt Men's Conference, FBC Chipley, Chipley, FL, United States.

Chapter 9—Faith: Our God Never Fails

[39] Merriam-Webster. (n.d.). Faith. In *Merriam-Webster.com dictionary*. Retrieved February 15, 2021, from https://www.merriam-webster.com/dictionary/faith

[40] Hughes, R. K. (2015). *Hebrews: An anchor for the soul*. Crossway. p. 288.

[41] *What does Hebrews 11:1 mean?* (n.d.). Got Questions. Retrieved February 15, 2021, from https://www.bibleref.com/Hebrews/11/Hebrews-11-1.html

[42] Blue Letter Bible. (n.d.). Ânâq. In *Blue Letter Bible*. Retrieved February 23, 2021, from https://www.blueletterbible.org/lang/lexicon/lexicon.cfm?Strongs=H6061&t=NIV

[43] Blackaby, H. T., Blackaby, R., & King, C. V. (2008). *Experiencing God: Knowing and doing the will of God*. B&H Books.

Chapter 10—Spiritual Leadership: Christ's Ambassadors

[44] The John Maxwell Company. (2013, July 8). *7 factors that influence influence*. Retrieved February 16, 2021, from https://www.johnmaxwell.com/blog/7-factors-that-influence-influence

[45] Merriam-Webster. (n.d.). Ambassador. In *Merriam-Webster.com dictionary*. Retrieved February 15, 2021, from https://www.merriam-webster.com/dictionary/ambassador

[46] Dixon, F. (n.d.). *Ten qualifications for leadership*. Words of Life Ministries. Retrieved February 15, 2021, from https://www.wordsoflife.co.uk/bible-studies/study-7-ten-qualifications-for-leadership

[47] Brainy Quote. (n.d.). *Billy Graham quotes*. Retrieved February 16, 2021, from https://www.brainyquote.com/quotes/billy_graham_161989

[48] Berman, J. (2014, April 20). *The three essential Warren Buffet quotes to live by*. Forbes. Retrieved February 16, 2021, from https://www.forbes.com/sites/jamesberman/2014/04/20/the-three-essential-warren-buffett-quotes-to-live-by/?sh=46534d9b6543

[49] Britannica. (n.d.). Transitive law. In *Britannica*. Retrieved February 15, 2021, from https://www.britannica.com/topic/transitive-law

[50] Merriam-Webster. (n.d.). Humility. In *Merriam-Webster.com dictionary*. Retrieved February 15, 2021, from https://www.merriam-webster.com/dictionary/humility

[51] *The servant as leader*. (n.d.). Robert K. Greenleaf Center for Servant Leadership. Retrieved February 15, 2021, from https://www.greenleaf.org/what-is-servant-leadership

[52] *Leaders eat last*. (n.d.). Simon Sinek. Retrieved February 15, 2021, from https://simonsinek.com/product/leaders-eat-last

[53] Scrapbook.com. (n.d.). *God gave us two ears and one mouth, so we ought to listen twice as much as we speak*. Retrieved February 16, 2021, from https://www.scrapbook.com/quotes/doc/13165.html

[54] Long, H., & Van Dam, A. (2020, May 8). U.S. unemployment rate soars to 14.7 percent, the worst since the Depression era. *Washington Post*. Retrieved February 15, 2021, from https://www.washingtonpost.com/business/2020/05/08/april-2020-jobs-report

[55] Lehman, C. F. (2020, June 1). *The role of marriage in the suicide crisis*. Institute for Family Studies. Retrieved February 15, 2021, from https://ifstudies.org/blog/the-role-of-marriage-in-the-suicide-crisis

[56] Jones, J. (2019, April 18). *U.S. church membership down sharply in past two decades*. Gallup. Retrieved February 15, 2021, from https://news.gallup.com/poll/248837/church-membership-down-sharply-past-two-decades.aspx

Chapter 11—Husband: Prophet, Priest, and King

[57] *Marriage and divorce*. (n.d.). American Psychological Association. Retrieved February 15, 2021, from https://www.apa.org/topics/divorce#:~:text=Marriage%20%26%20divorce&text=They%20are%20also%20good%20for,subsequent%20marriages%20is%20even%20higher

[58] Dickler, J. (2018, July 2). *How millennials are getting smarter about marriage*. CNBC. Retrieved February 15, 2021, from https://www.cnbc.com/2018/07/02/more-millennials-sign-prenups-before-marriage.html

[59] Avvo. (2016). *2016 Annual relationship, marriage, and divorce survey: Final report*. Retrieved March 16, 2021, from https://marketing-assets.avvo.com/media-resources/avvo-research/2016/avvo_relationship_study_2016_final_report.pdf

[60] Morley, P. (2014). *The man in the mirror: Solving the 24 problems men face*. Zondervan. pp. 141-160.

[61] *The 8 benefits of praying with your spouse*. (n.d.). Family First. Retrieved February 15, 2021, from https://www.imom.com/8-benefits-praying-spouse/

[62] Blue Letter Bible. (n.d.). Agapaō. In *Blue Letter Bible*. Retrieved February 15, 2021, from https://www.blueletterbible.org/lang/lexicon/lexicon.cfm?Strongs=G25&t=NIV

[63] *Greek/Hebrew definitions: Ginōskō*. (n.d.). Church of the Great God. Retrieved February 15, 2021, from https://www.bibletools.org/index.cfm/fuseaction/Lexicon.show/ID/G1097/ginosko.htm

[64] Blue Letter Bible. (n.d.). Matthew Henry: Commentary on Ephesians 5.In *Blue Letter Bible*. Retrieved February 15, 2021, from https://www.blueletterbible.org/Comm/mhc/Eph/Eph_005.cfm?a=1102029

[65] Brainy Quote. (n.d.). *Martin Luther quotes*. Retrieved February 16, 2021, from https://www.brainyquote.com/quotes/martin_luther_151420

[66] Scott, S. B., Rhoades, G. K., Stanley, S. M., Allen, E. S., & Markman, H. J. (2013). Reasons for divorce and recollections of premarital intervention: Implications for improving relationship education. *Couple and Family Psychology: Research and Practice, 2*(2), 131–145.

Chapter 12—Husbands, Recapture Your First Love!

[67] Hodges, C. (2017). *The Daniel dilemma: How to stand firm and love well in a culture of compromise*. Thomas Nelson. p. 126.

[68] Evans, T. (2016). *Kingdom marriage: Connecting God's purpose with your pleasure*. Tyndale House Publishers. p. 72.

[69] Merriam-Webster. (n.d.). Conjugal rights. In *Merriam-Webster.com dictionary*. Retrieved February 24, 2021, from https://www.merriam-webster.com/dictionary/conjugal%20rights

[70] *Does a woman always bleed when she has sex for the first time?* (2018, August 20). NHS England. Retrieved February 15, 2021, from https://www.nhs.uk/common-health-questions/sexual-health/does-a-woman-always-bleed-when-she-has-sex-for-the-first-time

[71] CNBC. (2015, January 20). *Things are looking up in America's porn industry*. Retrieved February 15, 2021, from https://www.nbcnews.com/business/business-news/things-are-looking-americas-porn-industry-n289431

[72] Patterson, R., & Price, J. (2012). Pornography, religion, and the happiness gap: Does pornography impact the actively religious differently? *Journal for the Scientific Study of Religion, 51*(1), 79-89.

[73] Brody, J. E. (2018, January 22). When a partner cheats. *The New York Times*. Retrieved February 15, 2021, from https://www.nytimes.com/2018/01/22/well/marriage-cheating-infidelity.html#:~:text=According%20to%20the%20American%20Association,relationships%20without%20intercourse%20are%20included.

[74] Beals, S. (2012, June 12). *Horizontal relationships expose our vertical relationship*. Joy-Filled Days. Retrieved February 24, 2021, from https://joyfilleddays.com/horizontal-relationships-expose-our-vertical-relationship

Chapter 14—A Father's Most Important Mission

[75] Blue Letter Bible. (n.d.). šānan. In *Blue Letter Bible*. Retrieved February 26, 2021, from https://www.blueletterbible.org/lang/lexicon/lexicon.cfm?Strongs=H8150&t=NIV

[76] Gospel Coalition. (2018). *The New City catechism for kids*. Crossway.

[77] Cannizzaro, M. (2012, June 17). Mickelson Sr. recalls how Phil learned game. *New York Post*. Retrieved February 18, 2021, from https://nypost.com/2012/06/17/mickelson-sr-recalls-how-phil-learned-game

[78] Blue Letter Bible. (n.d.). Matthew Henry: Commentary on Luke 11. In *Blue Letter Bible*. Retrieved February 15, 2021, from https://www.blueletterbible.org/Comm/mhc/Luk/Luk_011.cfm?a=984017

[79] Cited in Dobson. J. C. (1984). *Straight talk to men and their wives*. Word Books.

[80] Evans, T. (2014). *Raising kingdom kids*. Tyndale House Publishers. p. 122.

Chapter 15—Worker: Not About Me

[81] Morley, P. (2014). *The man in the mirror: Solving the 24 problems men face*. Zondervan. pp. 27-43.

Chapter 16—A New Mission for Work

[82] Sturt, D., & Nordstrom, T. (2018, March 8). 10 shocking workplace stats you need to know. *Forbes*. Retrieved February 15, 2021, from https://www.forbes.com/sites/davidsturt/2018/03/08/10-shocking-workplace-stats-you-need-to-know/?sh=7750429df3af

[83] Doyle, A. (2019, November 8). *How long should an employee stay at a job?* The Balance Careers. Retrieved February 15, 2021, from https://www.thebalancecareers.com/how-long-should-an-employee-stay-at-a-job-2059796#:~:text=How%20long%20does%20a%20typical,to%2034%20is%203.2%20years

[84] Goalcast. (n.d.). *C.S. Lewis quote: Integrity is doing the right thing even no one is watching*. Retrieved February 16, 2021, from https://www.goalcast.com/2018/03/26/15-c-s-lewis-quotes/c-s-lewis-quote1

Notes

[85] Merriam-Webster. (n.d.). Reverence synonyms. In *Merriam-Webster.com dictionary*. Retrieved February 27, 2021, from https://www.merriam-webster.com/dictionary/reverence#synonyms

[86] Belli, G. (2018, September 24). *46 percent of workers feel like they're underpaid. But are they?* PayScale. Retrieved February 15, 2021, from https://www.payscale.com/career-news/2018/09/46-percent-of-workers-feel-like-theyre-underpaid-but-are-they

Chapter 17—Friend: Two are Better than One

[87] Riggio, R. (2014, October 9). *How are men's friendships different from women's?* Psychology Today. Retrieved February 15, 2021, from https://www.psychologytoday.com/us/blog/cutting-edge-leadership/201410/how-are-men-s-friendships-different-women-s

[88] The Romans in Britain. (n.d.). *The Roman soldier's shield: The scutum*. Retrieved February 15, 2021, from https://www.romanobritain.org/8-military/mil_roman_soldier_shield.php

[89] Lawrence, T. (2018). *Find out who your friends are* [Song]. On *For the love* [Album]. Rocky Comfort Records.

[90] Blue Letter Bible. (n.d.). yāḏaʻ. In *Blue Letter Bible*. Retrieved February 27, 2021, from https://www.blueletterbible.org/lang/lexicon/lexicon.cfm?Strongs=H3045&t=NASB

[91] Evans, T. (2016). *Kingdom marriage: Connecting God's purpose with your pleasure*. Tyndale House Publishers. p. 135.

[92] Evans, T. (2016). *Kingdom marriage: Connecting God's purpose with your pleasure*. Tyndale House Publishers. p. 136.

[93] Blue Letter Bible. (n.d.). Matthew Henry: Commentary on Proverbs 20. In *Blue Letter Bible*. Retrieved February 15, 2021, from https://www.blueletterbible.org/Comm/mhc/Pro/Pro_020.cfm?a=648006

[94] Brainy Quote. (n.d.). *Helen Keller quotes*. Retrieved February 24, 2021, from https://www.brainyquote.com/quotes/helen_keller_382259

Chapter 18—Steward: It's all God's

[95] Hall, M. (2020). *Spiritual wealth: A 40-day journey*. Hallmarc Investments.

[96] Morley, P. (2014). *The man in the mirror: Solving the 24 problems men face*. Zondervan. p. 189.

[97] Dunn. R. (2007). *Faith crisis: What faith is and why it doesn't always do what you want*. David C. Cook. p. 184.

[98] Williams, P. R. (n.d.). *22 Christian quotes about money*. What Christians Want To Know. Retrieved February 16, 2021, from https://www.whatchristianswanttoknow.com/22-christian-quotes-about-money

[99] DavisFinancial. (2011, February 1). *I'm in debt up to my eyeballs*. [Video]. YouTube. https://www.youtube.com/watch?v=r0HX4a5P8eE

[100] Rose Publishing. (2016, February 8). *Trivia: How many verses in the Bible are about money?* Retrieved February 15, 2021, from https://blog.rose-publishing.com/2016/02/08/trivia-how-many-verses-in-the-bible-are-about-money/#.YBB3CuhKiUk

[101] Reference. (2020, March 28). *How much does a gallbladder weigh?* Retrieved March 19, 2021, from https://www.reference.com/science/much-gallbladder-weigh-a43debd533b0b22b

[102] Willis. A. (1997). *MasterLife: A biblical process for growing disciples*. Lifeway Christian Resources. p. 114.

[103] Casting Crowns. (2018). *Only Jesus* [Song]. On *Only Jesus* [Album]. Provident Label Group.

Conclusion—Burn the Ships

[104] David, L., Seinfeld, J., & Cowan. A. (Writers), & Cherones, T. (Director). (May 19, 1994). The opposite. (Season 5, Episode 22). [TV series episode]. In L. David, G. Shapiro, & H. West (Executive Producers), *Seinfeld*. Shapiro/West Productions; Castle Rock Entertainment.

[105] Henley, J. (2018, May 31). *Burn your ships: A history lesson about how to be a great leader*. The Center for Sales Strategy. Retrieved February 15, 2021, from https://blog.thecenterforsalesstrategy.com/burn-your-ships-how-to-be-a-great-leader#:~:text=In%20the%20year%201519%2C%20Hern,conquest%20of%20the%20Aztec%20empire.&text=We%20need%20to%20burn%20the%20ships

Made in the USA
Columbia, SC
27 June 2021